NAMES OF WOMEN OF THE BIBLE

JULIE-ALLYSON IERON

MOODY PRESS

CHICAGO

To John and Joyce Ieron,
my loving parents,
whose prayers, encouragement, and tireless support
made this book possible

CONTENTS

ACKNOWLEDGMENTS

Throughout my writing career, many talented friends have come alongside me. Although I could not possibly name all of them, a few special individuals warrant mention: Arlo and Helen Newell for making possible my work with Warner Press; Holly Miller, Gloria Gaither, and Sandra Lovely for nurturing my writing dream while I was attending Anderson University; Hank Nuwer, Beverley Pitts, and Earl Conn of Ball State University; Donald Anderson of the Baptist General Conference; and countless others. Thank you, my friends, for encouraging me along the journey.

Now I offer a special thank-you to my "today" friends at Moody Press, who in a tangible way made this book possible: Dennis Shere, Greg Thornton, and Jim Bell, who invited me to write this book; Bill Soderberg, who shepherded it through the editing process; and my very talented editor, Cheryl Dunlop.

Finally, I acknowledge the many friends who prayed for and with me as I undertook this project. May this book be as encouraging to you as it has been to me while I have prepared it.

1

INTRODUCTION:
CALL HER "WOMAN"

> Then the Lord God made a woman from the rib he had taken out of the man, and he brought her to the man. The man said, "This is now bone of my bones and flesh of my flesh; she shall be called 'woman,' for she was taken out of man." (*Genesis 2:22–23*)

The year was 1498. A twenty-three-year-old artist made a 150-mile trek from Rome to Carrara, an almost nameless village on the Ligurian Sea. According to his own word, he had been commissioned to sculpt "the most beautiful work in marble which exists today in Rome."[1] Only the highest quality of marble would do. And that meant Carraran marble. He would make the journey himself to assure its quality.

The artist worked with great intensity on the huge block of marble. Relentlessly, he chiseled away the excess to uncover the exceptional beauty locked within—a man and a woman. A woman of stunning delicacy, her facial features lovingly created, the detail amazingly lifelike, down to the wrinkles in her garment, the helpless gesture of her left hand, the angle of her bowed head that depicted her grief.

And the man. A symbolic representation of the shed earthly shell of the man of sorrows, intimately acquainted with grief. Eyes closed in death. Full-grown but—reminiscent of days gone by—cradled one last time in his mother's loving arm.

Michelangelo toiled tirelessly for three years to fashion this life-sized depiction of the Savior in the arms of Mary. Arguably one of the most distinctively beautiful works in marble ever created, his *Pietà* (translation: pity or compassion) resides in St. Peter's in Vatican City.

A woman and a man—lifelike yet lifeless— were formed of the finest marble with tender care by the hands of an artist, who was gifted to be a "cocreator" in the tradition of the only Creator capable of breathing life into His work.

God *spoke* many things into existence. Day. Night. Air. Seas. Land. Countless living creatures to be fruitful, multiply, and fill His creation. But when it came to the crowning achievements of His world, when it came to the creation of man and woman, He became intimately involved. Forming them with His own hand, breathing into them His own life. His touch created a deep and spiritual connection with them.

And from the Creator's perspective, it wasn't just good, it was "very good."

As with everything in creation, these two creatures each had a special purpose to fulfill. Together. And separately.

The man, He created out of the "dust of the ground"; the woman, He created out of the man's rib. As Matthew Henry notes, "The woman was made out of a rib out of the side of Adam; not made out of his head to rule over him, nor out of his feet to be trampled upon by him, but out of his side to be equal with him, under his arm to be protected, and near his heart to be beloved."[2]

The woman's purpose was to be partner and

companion with the man. She was to have her own identity and make her own choices. She had an intrinsic value, having been created in God's image as had the man.

God gave her a tender, nurturing heart. Because of her tragic choice to sin, her heart was to be pierced by *pietà*, even as His own would be pierced by her *pietà* at the Cross—yet another connection between mankind and the loving Creator.

God's work through the women of His creation is what we will study and celebrate in these pages. We will learn to know by name women who alternately display His grace or show the desperate need for His *pietà* in this fallen, groaning world.

And in so doing, we will honor the Creator, who not only chiseled and caressed our bodies, but conceived a way to redeem our souls.

NOTES

1. Frederick Hartt, *History of Italian Renaissance Art* (Englewood Cliffs, N.J.: Prentice-Hall, 1986), 470–71.

2. Genesis 2:21–25 from Matthew Henry's Commentary on the Whole Bible: New Modern Edition database © 1991, 1994 by Hendrickson Publishers, Inc

2

HANNAH:
GRACE

I am a woman who is deeply troubled. . . . I was pouring out my soul to the Lord. (*1 Samuel 1:15*)

It was to be three weeks of bliss. The trip of a life-time.

I had been chosen to join a touring choir on a mission to Europe. My dear friend Paul Yerden (our church's minister of music) and his wife, Rita Jo, would lead the tour.

While in Germany, we enjoyed the hospitality of host churches. They served us delicious cold cuts and cheese with heavily buttered hard rolls. Every afternoon we stopped at out-of-the-way bakeries for a stretch break and to enjoy luscious cream-filled pastries.

Soon after our arrival, my stomach began to complain. At first it was just a little discomfort, then the pain increased. I missed several concerts, having to lie down backstage while my friends were out front ministering. Discouragement crept in. It wasn't until five years later that my physician discovered the milk allergy—to cream, cheese, butter—that caused these symptoms. All I knew at the time was that I was missing all the good stuff by being sick.

One afternoon Rita Jo pushed a folded piece of

paper into my hand. On it she had handwritten the words to the hymn "He Giveth More Grace." I read and reread those words, contemplating their meaning, desiring the grace they bespoke.

Hannah, whose name means *grace,* came to know that grace intimately during her deep distress. She experienced the miracle-working grace of God, because she carried her burden right to Him.

Hannah had good reason to be depressed. You and I certainly would have been troubled in her circumstance. Peninnah, her husband's other wife, had many children; Hannah had none. Peninnah, the Scriptures say, tormented her rival for Elkanah's attention: "Whenever Hannah went up to the house of the Lord, her rival provoked her till she wept and would not eat" (1 Samuel 1:7). In her pain and in utter disregard for anyone who might be watching, Hannah bared her soul to the Lord, begging Him to give her a son, vowing to give that child back to Him for His service.

In response, the Scriptures record a beautiful phrase, "and the Lord remembered her" (1 Samuel 1:19). She touched the Father's heart with her tears and prayers, and He extended His hand to her. God honored Hannah's sincerity and fervency. He granted her not only that baby, but later He also gave her other sons and daughters.

The *American Heritage Dictionary* defines grace as "A favor rendered by one who need not do so." God acted graciously on Hannah's behalf, not because He was obligated to do so, but because He chose to do so. Moreover, He displayed His graciousness *through* her, by using her firstborn son (whom she named Samuel, which means, "heard of

God") to rule His people in justice and honor. In his old age, long after his mother was gone, Samuel had the privilege of anointing Israel's greatest king, David.

Hannah's response to the Lord's provision was as exemplary as her request. First, she did as she had promised. She gave the child Samuel to minister in the Lord's temple to become a blessing back to the Lord. Second, she gave all the glory to God, her heart overflowing into a poetic prayer of acknowledgment and thanks. "My heart rejoices in the Lord; in the Lord my horn is lifted high. . . . There is no one holy like the Lord; there is no one besides you; there is no Rock like our God" (1 Samuel 2:1–2).

In some obvious ways, we are unlike Hannah. In few of our homes do two wives of the same man live together (although if they did, feuding would not be unthinkable). And in our culture, inability to have children is not thought to be a curse from God, as it was in Hannah's day.

But in the ways that count, we are very much alike. Our needs, our heavy burdens, the demands of life, and our tormentors and problems too often threaten to overwhelm us. Like I did on my college bus trip, we often suffer alone, when with just a prayer we can call upon the one who will "remember us" as He remembered Hannah all those centuries ago.

The writer of Proverbs noted that God "mocks proud mockers but gives grace to the humble" (3:34). It is a truth James quotes in his epistle (4:6).

It was in humbly pouring out her heart to God that Hannah found her burden lifted. Her life can be an example to us of what God can do—if we do our part. We are told in Scripture what that part is: "Let us then approach the throne of grace with confidence, so that we may receive mercy and find grace to help us in our time of need" (Hebrews 4:16).

It has been many years since Rita Jo handed me that paper, but I'll never forget its effect upon me. Those words reminded me that God, through His only Son Jesus whom He graciously sacrificed to meet the ultimate need of humanity, stands ready to provide for all my needs through His abundant, overflowing supply. And He does this not because of any obligation, but because He chooses to do so.

My dear, loving Father, I need a portion of that overflowing supply of grace today, and I know so many others around me have that same need. Please provide for me, and equip me to be a conduit of Your grace in the lives of those I love. Amen.

3

ABIGAIL:
MY FATHER IS JOY

David said to Abigail, "Praise be to the Lord, the God of Israel, who has sent you today to meet me. May you be blessed for your good judgment." *(1 Samuel 25:32–33a)*

Rob and his wife, Joanna, are having a baby. Their first child, a son, is two and a half. Rob and his son giggle and wrestle and share ice cream cones. Rob and Joanna just learned their second child is going to be a girl. Now Rob is nervous. *What do I know about girls?* he wonders. *I've never even had a sister. How can I be a good father to her?*

Rob is neither the first nor the last father to pose that question.

But somewhere between her birth and adulthood, Rob's little girl, like tens of thousands before her, will win her daddy's heart. She will be a source of joy and gladness to her parents as they raise her in the knowledge of the Lord. Their bonds of love and respect and interdependence will be strengthened with each passing year.

When my friend Debbie got married a few years ago, she asked me to sing "Daddy's Little Girl" as part of her special day. Shared memories paraded before the glistening eyes of both father and daughter as I sang the words. This bride was proud to have brought joy to her father, and she wanted to acknowledge that special relationship as she moved into her new life with her husband.

Certainly just being a loving daughter brings joy to her parents' lives. But a daughter can enhance that joy by living a life of obedience to her heavenly Father, of fearing Him, of making consistently wise choices even against difficult odds.

Abigail, whose story begins in 1 Samuel 25, lived a life consistent with her name, *my father is joy* (an alternate translation is *the father's joy*). Let's peer into the pages that record her story.

While Saul was still reigning as king of Israel, God's favor departed from him, resting instead on David. Although David could have killed Saul on more than one occasion, David believed it was not his place to be the one to bring about Saul's demise. Instead, David and his followers ran for their lives, hiding out in the desert of Maon. They provided protection for the flocks and servants of a rich man named Nabal. When it came time for Nabal's flocks to be sheared, David (the nation's rightful king), asked for a small portion of the food from the feast to feed his men. Nabal, whom the Bible calls "surly and mean in his dealings" (1 Samuel 25:3), bitterly refused to provide a morsel of food to David.

This infuriated David the warrior, who determined to slaughter Nabal and his household.

Fortunately, a discerning servant explained the situation to Nabal's wife, Abigail, a woman of "good judgment." What was the response of this wise woman when she heard David was coming with four hundred armed men? "Abigail lost no time. She took two hundred loaves of bread, two skins of wine, five dressed sheep, five seahs of roasted grain, a hun-

dred cakes of raisins and two hundred cakes of
pressed figs, and loaded them on donkeys" (1 Samuel 25:18).

Then she sent her servants on ahead and
mounted her own donkey—all the while neglecting
to tell Nabal of her intentions. When she overtook
David and his band, Abigail bowed down before
David, begging him to listen to her plea:

> *May my lord pay no attention to that wicked man Nabal. He is just like his name—his name is Fool, and folly*
> *goes with him. But as for me, your servant, I did not see*
> *the men my master sent. . . . And let this gift, which your*
> *servant has brought to my master, be given to the men*
> *who follow you.* (1 Samuel 25:25, 27)

With a final stroke of genius, the wise Abigail
completed her argument and appealed to David's
sense of justice by telling him, "Let no wrongdoing
be found in you as long as you live" (1 Samuel 25:28).

Abigail's actions bring to mind the proverb,
"The wise woman builds her house, but with her
own hands the foolish one tears hers down" (Proverbs
14:1). Her actions also echo Proverbs 31:26: "She
speaks with wisdom, and faithful instruction is on
her tongue."

Her contrite countenance and soothing words
appeased David's anger. He called off his assassination and demolition crew, and Abigail returned
home to her evil husband. When Nabal learned
how near to disaster he had placed himself, he literally had a stroke. Within days, he died.

Soon Abigail, who had proven herself valuable
by her discretion and wise counsel, became David's
wife.

Although the Bible doesn't record her father's name, it shows Abigail as a woman of calm judgment in the face of impending doom—a daughter any father would be joyful to have raised, in Bible times or in modern days.

My Lord, teach me to conduct myself with discretion and calm judgment. Help me to recognize danger and to act wisely, in accordance with Your will. Amen.

4

QUEEN OF SHEBA:
ROYAL

> When the queen of Sheba heard about the
> fame of Solomon and his relation to the name
> of the Lord, she came to test him with hard
> questions. *(1 Kings 10:1a)*

What are the qualities of a good leader? How should a godly woman in a position of responsible leadership conduct herself? Where can she go to obtain wise counsel? After whom can she pattern herself?

When I was promoted into a position managing a department, I was awash in these questions. My experience had brought me to this logical next step. It was clear that the Lord was leading my superiors to make the offer and leading me to accept the position. And yet, I felt somewhat vulnerable, even unworthy.

I looked to others who were already in similar positions. Unfortunately, even in this generation, positive role models for women in management are few. Some women become tyrants, becoming as aggressive as any male dictator has ever been; others turn to a distorted brand of femininity—never stating their opinions, acting overly submissive, allowing themselves to be dominated.

Being somewhat moderate in temperament, I sought examples of those who had taken the middle ground—like Goldilocks in the bears' home

—looking for the qualities that would make me "just right" as a manager: not too domineering, not too wimpy. After some searching I did locate a manager who exuded femininity but was respected as the quintessential professional—by her peers, superiors, and subordinates, and even by her competitors.

One evening I sat in my studio with notepad in hand, listing her professional qualities: compassionate, transparent, encouraging, calm, insightful, attentive, trusting, trustworthy, forgiving, decisive, persistent. . . . As I looked over the page, one word seemed to be at the root of every character quality: *wise.*

Wise—like Solomon. Yes. That was it. When young King Solomon took the reins of power, he asked God for wisdom, "Give your servant a discerning heart to govern your people and to distinguish between right and wrong. For who is able to govern this great people of yours?" (1 Kings 3:9).

It was Solomon's wisdom (for God granted his request, being pleased with its intent) that drew a royal entourage from a kingdom to the south of Israel (probably Arabia or northern Africa) to Solomon's courts. At the head of the entourage was the nation's sovereign ruler, known to posterity only as the queen of Sheba.

This woman, who knew the yoke of power as well as any royal could, journeyed to Israel in search of wisdom.

When the queen of Sheba heard of Solomon's fame, she came to Jerusalem to test him with hard questions. Ar-

*riving with a very great caravan—with camels carrying
spices, large quantities of gold, and precious stones—she
came to Solomon and talked with him about all she had
on her mind. Solomon answered all her questions; nothing was too hard for him to explain to her.* (2 Chronicles
9:1–2)

Here was another manager to emulate, another
woman to hold as a role model. For she realized
how much she did not know. She thought through
her "hard questions," perhaps listing them out on a
scroll, accumulating them over the course of years
of ruling her country. She made no pretense of om-
niscience, as so many leaders would have done.
Her country was a strong commercial power whose
trade specialties were perfumes and incense. When
in the course of international trade she heard stories of Solomon's great wisdom, she considered the
cost of the journey but a pittance in the light of
having her questioning heart satisfied.

To his credit, Solomon patiently answered her
questions. He treated her with the dignity befitting
her position—meeting her admiration and satisfy-
ing her curiosity. Not only did he regale her with
his wisdom, but Solomon also introduced her to
the Lord his God, giving the glory back to its original source.

Once her questions were satisfied, the queen
made this speech: "Praise be to the Lord your God,
who has delighted in you and placed you on his
throne as king to rule for the Lord your God. Because of the love of your God for Israel and his
desire to uphold them forever, he has made you
king over them, to maintain justice and righteousness" (2 Chronicles 9:8).

Following that train of thought, the only infallible source of wisdom is God Himself. It was He who equipped Solomon for the task to which he was called. It was He who used Solomon to reveal Himself to the searching heart of the queen of Sheba. And this same God will equip you and me with enough wisdom—in fact, with all the necessary qualifications—for the tasks to which He calls us.

Lord, give me the humility and clear-mindedness to realize how much I do not know. Bring into my life people who can teach me what I need to know. Keep me aware that all the glory for that which I do know belongs to You. Amen.

5

HULDAH:
GLIDES SWIFTLY

She said to them, "This is what the Lord, the
God of Israel, says . . ." (2 Kings 22:15)

To most onlookers, Nannie would have been an
unlikely counselor. In the years I knew her, she
seldom left the confines of her South Florida home
(although I did coerce her out to a restaurant for
dinner twice). Her world consisted of endless
housework (including creating lip-smacking deli-
cacies in her muggy little kitchen), TV, daily news-
papers, and a Bible. Oh yes, and the chair where
her arthritic legs knelt and prayed for hours each
day.

Her dedicated Bible reading and consistent
prayer life were the two elements that equipped her
to dispense wise counsel. To this day, I praise God
that I listened to His voice clearly audible in the lilt-
ing tones of my Nannie's accent.

Just as she listened for the Lord's voice, she listened intently when I poured out my heart. Nannie
was the first to grab hold of the vision of my becoming a journalist and a public speaker. I
remember the sticky afternoon during my college
spring break when she looked up from reading the
newspaper, pointed to the woman on the TV screen
(a Christian interviewer), and announced, "Julie,

you should do that." She had recognized qualities in me that I had been too afraid to acknowledge in myself. That this woman with a hot line to heaven believed in me provided me with the courage to take the risk to follow God's plan for my life. We talked long into the evening about my hopes and dreams. She caught the vision. She prayed for and with me.

Back in the dorm only a few months later, I received a late-night phone call. The *dreaded* late-night phone call. My mom's tearful voice was on the other end. "It's Nannie. She lay down this afternoon after preparing lunch for your aunt, and she never woke up. She's with Jesus."

Nannie's death was a potent reminder of the fleeting nature of life. There had been no warning that we could see. That's too often how life is.

There was a woman in Scripture, Huldah, whose name reflected that same concept: life glides by swiftly, fleetingly. Actually, Huldah means *weasel* (not exactly a flattering name), but the concept comes from a root word that refers to the animal's quick, gliding motion.

Huldah's husband served as keeper of the wardrobe in King Josiah's royal court. But it was she who was well-known in the court for her gift of prophecy. Obviously, God in His providence planted her in that place at that time. She was a contemporary of the prophets Jeremiah and Zephaniah. Yet for some reason when King Josiah sent messengers to inquire of the Lord, God led them to Huldah, who lived a few buildings away from the royal palace.

In his commentary on 2 Kings 22:11–20,

Matthew Henry explains their probable reasoning this way: "They had had more and longer acquaintance with her and greater assurances of her commission than of any other; they had, it is likely, consulted her upon other occasions, and had found that the word of God in her mouth was truth."[1]

Huldah had proven trustworthy over a lifetime of ministry. Not intimidated by the difficult message given her to deliver, she spoke the word of the Lord with courage and conviction. She instructed the messengers to tell the king that God's wrath would indeed fall on his kingdom because of the people's unfaithfulness to the covenant He had made with them. But she assured them that God was pleased with Josiah's softness of heart:

> *"Because your heart was responsive and you humbled yourself before the Lord when you heard what I have spoken against this place and its people, that they would become accursed and laid waste, and because you tore your robes and wept in my presence, I have heard you, declares the Lord. Therefore I will gather you to your fathers, and you will be buried in peace. Your eyes will not see all the disaster I am going to bring on this place." So they took her answer back to the king.* (2 Kings 22:19–20)

She spoke faithfully what she heard from God. Note that God entrusted a woman with this challenging, convicting message. A woman was His mouthpiece of choice to advise this God-fearing king. And in His ultimate stamp of approval, God's word through Huldah proved true.

Huldah glides swiftly through Scripture, mentioned only this once—a reminder that God will use the servant He chooses, that a lifetime of faithfulness may yield but one memorable moment. Yet that one moment, buttressed by a lifetime of faithful service, can make an eternal difference.

Few people know the names of those who led Chuck Swindoll or Tony Evans or Kay Arthur to the Lord. But the fruits of their ministries continue to make memorable changes in thousands of lives in our generation. Be assured that whether posterity remembers or forgets them, the Lord will honor His faithful servants.

I think of those who have carried His Word into my life, each leaving as a legacy a lifetime of faithful service to God. People like my parents and grandparents, Sunday school teachers, college professors, and especially my Nannie. Although her life on this earth is over, her legacy of faithfulness lives on in our family members, whose lives she touched in countless memorable moments.

Loving Lord, thank You for those who have glided through my life, encouraging me to follow You. Those who have challenged me to walk more closely with You. Those who have delivered Your Word, even when it was a difficult word to hear. May my fleeting life leave that kind of imprint on those I touch. Amen.

NOTE

1. Matthew Henry's Commentary on the Whole Bible: New Modern Edition database © 1991, 1994 by Hendrickson Publishers, Inc.

6

JEHOSHEBA:
JEHOVAH IS HER OATH

> But Jehosheba, the daughter of King
> Jehoram, took Joash son of Ahaziah and stole
> him away from among the royal princes who
> were about to be murdered and put him and
> his nurse in a bedroom. (2 Chronicles 22:11)

Is there hope for kids in this generation? That
question has been asked about "today's youth" by
members of every older generation since time began. In this sin-filled world we see deterioration,
for by nature men and women are slaves to sin.
That nature at times causes an entire generation to
sink to an all-time low, a little deeper in the quag-
mire than the previous generation.

This week I met a twenty-five-year veteran of
the teaching profession. He has seen generations
come and go through the doors of his public high
school journalism classroom in south-suburban
Chicagoland. I doubt whether he's a believer in
Christ.

Wanting a secular perspective, I asked him if
this generation of kids is as different on the inside
as they seem on the outside. "Yes," he replied sadly.
"These kids have more pressures than I can remember any other generation having. Their problems
are more intense; they are serious, life-problems. To
escape their pressures, they turn to alcohol in a
tragic way." He relayed the story of a promising
young cheerleader whose friends dared her to guz-

zle so much hard liquor at one time that she died from alcohol poisoning.

After a pause, I asked, "So, then, are they without hope?"

"No," he said. "Those who come from religious families of all backgrounds seem to be better adjusted, more grounded somehow. These kids have the best odds. But then there are some who have all the odds against them—they come from broken homes, abusive situations, terrible problems, and yet they succeed despite the odds. So, there is hope for these kids." That hope has sustained my friend through all the difficult years he has encountered in his profession.

As I thought about high school kids who succeed despite the odds, I began to consider an obscure young woman in the Bible who did that. In fact, through her, God preserved David's royal line from annihilation. Her name was Jehosheba, *Jehovah is her oath*.

Jehosheba was a princess, the daughter of Judah's King Jehoram, but hers was no fairy-tale existence. Her world was awash in the blood of murdered family members, godless worship, and evil alliances.

Her grandfather was Jehoshaphat, a king who followed most of Jehovah's commands (2 Chronicles 17:3). Unfortunately, her father Jehoram was an evil king who allied himself with Israel's King Ahab by marrying his daughter Athaliah. Jehoram heartlessly murdered all of his brothers to establish his uncontested throne. The Scriptures are unclear as to whether Ahab's daughter was Jehosheba's mother. (The kings took many wives.)

His reign was so perverse that it was only God's promise to David that kept Jehoram's family alive: "The Lord was not willing to destroy the house of David. He had promised to maintain a lamp for him and his descendants forever" (2 Chronicles 21:7).

During this chaotic reign of terror, Princess Jehosheba married a godly man, Jehoiada, a faithful priest in God's temple. Unbeknownst to them at the time, this marriage was part of God's providential salvation of David's family line.

Jehosheba's older brothers were all killed by raiders, and only her youngest brother Ahaziah (son of Ahab's daughter Athaliah) survived. Their father Jehoram died at age forty of a painful intestinal disease. When Jehoram died, the Scripture records: "He passed away, to no one's regret, and was buried in the City of David, but not in the tombs of the kings" (2 Chronicles 21:20). The people of Judah crowned Ahaziah king.

Ahaziah also did evil in God's sight and reigned only one year. During a visit to neighboring Israel, Ahaziah was killed by God's men who were destroying the entire house of his grandfather Ahab. Back in Judah, Queen Athaliah seized the kingdom. She slaughtered everyone in the royal family.

But God brought Jehosheba into the palace at the right time and gave her the opportunity to hide her nephew Joash, Ahaziah's infant son, in a bedroom. Endangering their own lives, Jehosheba and her husband brought the boy to God's temple, where they hid and raised him.

For six years Athaliah made a mockery of ruling the kingdom—she sank so low as to break into

God's temple and use the sacred objects to worship pagan gods. By contrast, Jehosheba and Jehoiada were godly people; they taught Prince Joash the ways of God. When the time was right, they established Joash as rightful king. He was a godly king as long as Jehoiada was alive. Unfortunately, when the priest died, the king surrounded himself with godless advisers, to his downfall.

No twentieth-century action movie could have been more gory, more heart-pounding than Jehosheba's life story. She had every excuse to have turned out as evil as her surroundings. Think of all she endured: a wicked stepmother, a father so cruel that no one grieved when he died prematurely, assassinated siblings, a life of hiding. Consider, too, that Jehosheba had more right to the throne than Athaliah. With Joash dead, she would have been the last in David's line.

Nevertheless, Jehosheba was a credit to her prophetic name. Instead of acting selfishly, this young woman went against her family's grain when she acted in a way befitting all true people of God. Princess Jehosheba became a willing servant in God's hands—what her hands found to do, she did heartily so that God's reputation was enhanced.

With the help of *Jehovah is her oath,* God proved Himself faithful to His oath: He spared the royal line of the Messiah, using this princess who had grown up godly despite living in an evil world.

God, teach me to be as unselfish as Jehosheba was. May I be more concerned with Your glory and Your reputation than my own comfort. Amen.

7

ESTHER/HADASSAH:
STAR/MYRTLE

> And the king loved Esther more than all the
> women, and she found favor and kindness
> with him more than all the virgins, so that he
> set the royal crown on her head and made her
> queen instead of Vashti. (*Esther 2:17 NASB*)

Stars captivate us.

Check with the U.S. government's budget office, where you'll find billions of tax dollars allocated to space exploration. When the Russian Space Station Mir with three people aboard has a fender bender, it is global news. When the space shuttle blasts off from Cape Canaveral, it is carried live on network television.

In 1997 scientists began receiving transmissions from the surface of Mars from Rover. Drab photos of sandy-colored rock not only made front-page news, but became the subject of an evening's live programming on CNN and adorned one of the most visited Web sites on the Internet.

Or note this: The *Star Wars* trilogy was re-released, and throngs flocked to theaters to "see it again for the first time." *Star Trek* not only continues to draw viewers after twenty years, but it has spawned blockbuster movies and three popular spin-off series.

Space and its resident stars are bigger than life.

Down on earth, we're fascinated by people whom we perceive to shine like the stars—stars created not by God's almighty hand but by spin-doctors and public relations specialists. These people seem to have superhuman abilities or outstanding beauty or an inordinate amount of financial power. We dream of emulating these stars. We pattern our lives after theirs in the hopes that we may attain their heights.

Unfortunately, the light from many of these is more akin to the short-lived "rockets' red glare" than to the consistent light from the heavens that has journeyed countless years to reach the earth's atmosphere and enliven the evening sky. Sadly, most human stars lose their light appeal when we encounter their humanity head-on.

The Bible records a star of the human variety who did not fall off her celestial perch. Esther—*star*. A woman outstanding in beauty. A woman who became queen of a great empire. A woman who displayed the shining character traits of loyalty, obedience, and wisdom. A star worth emulating.

Esther's story took place while Nehemiah's crew was rebuilding Jerusalem's walls and temple. Before Israel's exile, Isaiah and Jeremiah had implored God's people to return to their homeland after seventy years. Although some Israelites returned to the Promised Land, Mordecai, the cousin who raised the orphan Esther, was among the many who chose not to return. Esther's account displays God's hand in protecting His people from evil, even when they did not heed His command.

Persian King Xerxes (Ahasuerus in some translations) had removed Queen Vashti (see chapter 14) from her exalted position. He called for a kingdom-wide search for beautiful virgins to be placed in his harem and pampered with twelve months of aromatic beauty treatments in preparation for one night with him. If one of these women pleased him, she would become queen.

Esther was a pure young woman with a sweet countenance, lovely to behold. Her Israelite name was Hadassah, which means *myrtle*—a fragrant Mediterranean floral shrub whose fruits are darkly colored berries. She lived with Mordecai, a keeper at the palace gate, in the royal city of Susa (150 miles north of the Persian Gulf in modern-day Iran). When Esther was taken to the palace, she immediately caught the attention of the person in charge of the harem:

> Esther also was taken to the king's palace and entrusted to Hegai, who had charge of the harem. The girl pleased him and won his favor. Immediately he provided her with her beauty treatments and special food. He assigned to her seven maids selected from the king's palace and moved her and her maids into the best place in the harem. (Esther 2:8b–9)

She wasn't finished turning heads. "When the turn came for Esther . . . to go to the king, she asked for nothing other than what Hegai, the king's eunuch who was in charge of the harem, suggested. And Esther won the favor of everyone who saw her" (Esther 2:15). Xerxes included. Soon, the orphan Hadassah was transformed into the lovely Queen Esther.

Some years later, the king's wicked adviser Haman concocted a plan to purge the empire of all Jews, especially of Mordecai, a nemesis who would not bow when Haman passed by. The king signed Haman's plan into law.

Esther, snugly ensconced in the cocoon of palace life (with her national origin hidden at Mordecai's instruction) heard that Mordecai was in mourning. She sent her trusted messenger to her weeping cousin and received back the story—with Mordecai's audacious request: to go "into the king's presence to beg for mercy and plead with him for her people" (4:8).

Even for the queen, the penalty for approaching the king unbidden was nothing less than death, unless he extended his golden scepter and invited her in. But Mordecai reminded Esther, "Do not think that because you are in the king's house you alone of all the Jews will escape. For if you remain silent at this time, relief and deliverance for the Jews will arise from another place, but you and your father's family will perish. And who knows but that you have come to royal position for such a time as this?" (Esther 4:13–14).

Esther resolutely replied: "Go, gather together all the Jews who are in Susa, and fast for me. Do not eat or drink for three days, night or day. I and my maids will fast as you do. When this is done, I will go to the king, even though it is against the law. And if I perish, I perish" (4:16).

God's name is never used in the account of Esther, nor is prayer specifically mentioned. However, by implication, the fasting may have included prayer; certainly God's hand was in the deliverance of His people.

The king, pleased to see his queen, extended the scepter and granted her request of a private audience with him and Haman over dinner in her apartment. Her request that night was for a second dinner the next night. On the night of the threesome's second dinner, Esther identified herself as a Jew, begging the king for her own life and for that of her people. The king had Haman arrested and killed, and he allowed the Jews to defend themselves from their enemies. Esther's cousin Mordecai was elevated from doorkeeper to chief adviser, in place of Haman.

Throughout this account we see Esther winning the favor of those in authority. A quiet, submissive spirit; obedient actions; and wise choices made her stand out from her society, even as it would make each of us stand out today. In a time when many of her people had forsaken their God-given heritage (sound familiar?), Esther displayed faith and courage, risking her own comfort for the sake of a higher call.

She lived up to her Israelite name (in fragrant beauty and fruitfulness) and her Persian name, being a star aptly suspended in space, willingly used by God's hand for the deliverance of His people. Can we do any less for our generation?

Lord, this world is dark with many enemies lurking in the shadows. Help me to shine with Your heavenly light, revealing Your truth to those around me. Make me willing to face the consequences of becoming a brilliant star for You. Amen.

ELIZABETH:
OATH OF GOD

Blessed is she who has believed that what
the Lord has said to her will be accomplished!
(*Luke 1:45*)

Sherm Swenson distinguished himself in the corporate world by his hard work. Early in his
career he received some advice from one who was
older and wiser: Never promise what you can't deliver; always deliver what you promise. That's integrity
in a nutshell.

Sherm's word became as good as an oath.
Whether popular or unpopular, whether it would
clinch or squelch a deal, Sherm told the truth.

As days went by, he noticed that fewer and fewer of the students who entered the workplace out of
business school held this ethical standard. They
seemed to be straying exponentially farther from
this code each year. Taking an early retirement from
corporate life, Sherm became a college administra-
tor. Out of concern for tomorrow's culture, he
began to mentor students, one small group a year.
He and his wife invited the groups into their home.
He met with them regularly to train them in the ele-
mentary but easily forgotten priority of honesty
above profit. His students considered themselves
honored to be learning from one with Sherm's reputation.

His example is a small copy of the one God sets forth in His Word. God is faithful and true. His promises are sure. His Word will stand, though all around may fall.

God has proven Himself by fulfilling His promises to His people down through the ages— like the promise He fulfilled to Elizabeth and her husband, Zechariah the priest. She and her husband were both commended for observing the commandments "blamelessly" and being "upright in the sight of God" (Luke 1:6).

How appropriate the name Elizabeth (*Oath of God*) was for this godly woman: She was one who received a promise from God and chose to believe Him.

When Zechariah was serving in the temple, he received word from the angel Gabriel that his wife, though previously unable to have children and "well along in years" (Luke 1:7), would conceive and bear a son. (It's amazing how many biblical accounts of the lives of women include a season of infertility, followed by the birth of a child of promise.)

When Zechariah doubted, he became unable to speak until the day the child was born. Elizabeth, on the other hand, was blessed; she had faith and she recognized it in others. Later she told her cousin Mary, who was to bear the Messiah, "Blessed is she who has believed that what the Lord has said to her will be accomplished!" (Luke 1:45). But Elizabeth also was blessed by God's faithfulness to His promise.

We don't hear much about blessing in our culture. Author and preacher Crawford Loritts notes that a Hebrew word translated in our Bibles as "blessed" in the Psalms actually could have been translated as "fulfilled." When we say we feel blessed, we usually mean we are feeling happy or content. How often are we happy or content or fulfilled? Certainly Elizabeth experienced those emotions when she received the blessing of her son, John, who was the one chosen to prepare the way for the coming Messiah.

Elizabeth and Zechariah were said to have consistently observed the Lord's commandments and regulations. This required an intimate knowledge of God's expectations and requirements, probably a daily "reality check" to be certain they were on track.

As we seek to become more like those whom Scripture commends as blameless, as we seek to know God's will by reading His Word, we will come to understand His promises to us—comforting promises He made for all believers of all times: "I will never leave you nor forsake you" (Hebrews 13:5 NKJV), "I know the plans I have for you" (Jeremiah 29:11), "My word . . . will not return to me empty, but will accomplish what I desire and achieve the purpose for which I sent it" (Isaiah 55:11).

The blessed, fulfilling life is one where I know God's promises and take Him at His word. Then I can follow in the path of those like Sherm, who is renowned for the dependability of his words.

Dear Lord, help me to know Your character so well that I believe the amazing promises You set forth in Scripture. Then let me be known as one whose promises can always be trusted. Amen.

ANNA:
INSPIRED WOMAN

There was also a prophetess, Anna, the
daughter of Phanuel, of the tribe of Asher. . . .
She never left the temple but worshiped night
and day, fasting and praying. (*Luke 2:36–37*)

Writing is the daughter of inspiration. And inspiration is the daughter of prayer.

So I have found in my years of writing. I cannot write anything with eternal value or life-
changing significance apart from prayer. I may be
able to dash off a few lines of mediocre copy on
meaningless topics without making them a matter
of time with the heavenly Father, but when I am
seeking to understand and communicate "kingdom
thoughts," I cannot do so apart from the Holy Spirit's guidance.

This is a truth I relearned this morning, as I la-
bored over how to describe the life and significance
of a godly woman about whom we know only the
minutest of details. I studied the Scripture, perused
the commentaries, read about the lifestyles of the
times. Yet I was no closer to knowing this woman
than before. It was then, at the end of my human
knowledge, that I prayed:

*God, You saw to it that Anna the prophetess would
be recorded in Scripture for us to know about. But there
is so little recorded; there is so much more I would have
wanted to know. You know her, Lord. You know every-*

*thing about her, inside and out, as You know everything
about me. Help me know what to say about Anna;
make her come alive through Your Scriptures, that we
may learn the lesson of love that kept her challenged
and inspired through multiple decades of constant
prayer and attendance in Your temple.*

Then I reread the Scripture with eyes of re-
newed faith. "She never left the temple but
worshiped night and day, fasting and praying."
Somewhere in her eighty-four years, most of them
spent as a widow (she had lived with her husband
only seven years before he died, and she had no
children), she had learned a priceless secret: Worship and prayer go hand in hand. There cannot be
true communion with God, true communication
with Him, without a proper understanding and awe
for who He is.

Pastor and author Joseph Carroll writes in the
introduction to his classic little book, *How to Worship Jesus Christ,* "The masters who have given
themselves to prayer agree, without discord, that
the most important element of all is the essential of
worship."[1]

King David knew this truth well. We read in
Psalm 27:4: "One thing I ask of the Lord, this is
what I seek: that I may dwell in the house of the
Lord all the days of my life, to gaze upon the beauty
of the Lord and to seek him in his temple." This
king had an appropriate response to the awesome
invitation to worship the Lord.

Anna spent every waking moment of her life in
worship. In prayer and in service, she did all to
God's glory. And so, she received the blessing of
God, divine inspiration. She was called a prophet-

ess, *an inspired woman.* She was among a limited company of godly prophetesses whose names are recorded in Scripture: Miriam, Deborah, Huldah, Anna.

While she is even now enjoying her heavenly reward for faithful service, we can glimpse a portion of Anna's earthly reward in Luke's Gospel. When Mary and Joseph brought the child Jesus to be dedicated at the temple in Jerusalem, it was Anna and a righteous, devout man—Simeon—who prophesied about the child, encouraging His parents by reaffirming God's unique calling for this young one and confirming (as if the angel's testimony and His miraculous conception needed confirmation) that He was the Messiah, God's divine source of salvation for all people.

Anna had the privilege of carrying the news to all those "who were looking forward to the redemption of Jerusalem" (Luke 2:38). She knew who they were—a community of servant-minded worshipers like herself. And they knew her. She knew they would listen to her report.

The prophetess Anna continues to inspire listening worshipers down through the millennia. Her example of selfless prayer and worshipful service challenges modern-day believers to renew our dedication to entering the Holy Place with awe-filled appreciation for the marvelous invitation offered to us by the Creator of the universe: to enter into His holy presence and make our requests known to Him.

Anna's name (like Hannah in chapter 1) means *grace.* God showed His grace toward her sacrifices of service and worship by allowing her the once-in-a-lifetime, immeasurable joy of attesting to His glory, of recognizing the promised Messiah, God's only begotten Son. What greater glory could she ever have attained? What sacrifice of time or effort, what ache or pain, what bodily hunger or thirst didn't pale in significance when compared to the incomparable experience of holding God in her arms?

With dividends like those Anna enjoyed, isn't a lifetime of prayer and worship dedicated to serving Jesus Christ worth any sacrifice we could ever make?

Lord, teach me to worship You; create in me a growing passion for the kind of prayerful service Anna offered up throughout her life. Let me do this expecting in return only the unparalleled joy of touching You, of knowing You, of loving You. Amen.

NOTE
1. Joseph S. Carroll, *How to Worship Jesus Christ* (Chicago: Moody, 1991), 11.

10

EVE:
LIFEGIVER

Adam named his wife Eve, because she
would become the mother of all the living.
(*Genesis 3:20*)

I love words. I love to try them on for size, to listen
to the sounds they make as I intone them. I love
to watch them make a once-dull page sparkle with
life. I love to make them dance on my tongue. But
there's one word I hated when I learned it: *ironic*.

I hated it because of its similarity to my last
name; in fact, stop short of the "ic" and you'll have the
pronunciation of Ieron almost exactly. (I know you've
been wondering how to say it; nearly everyone
does!) My grade-school companions used to play
with the word *ironic,* interchanging it with my last
name. I didn't think that wordplay was at all cute.

When I arrived in high school, I began to find a
new appreciation for *ironic*. As we studied great lit-
erature, I came to understand how many writers
used irony as an integral device of their plots.
Shakespeare was the master at this.

A brief overview of the plot of *Romeo and Juliet*
is rife with irony. Romeo's friend brings him to a
gala to make him forsake his attentions to a woman
who was not good for him. There he meets and falls
instantly in love with Juliet, the daughter of his
family's sworn enemy. Certainly, Juliet isn't good for

Romeo. Juliet quickly comes to return his love. The couple is married secretly. The two stage their own mock deaths to free themselves of their families' ties. Through several ironic twists, each thinks the other to be truly dead and thus commits suicide. You know the end of the tragedy: the young lovers are said to have been reunited in death.

Creative minds in Western culture didn't invent irony. In fact, irony in real life is as old as the creation of the world. Consider the first woman who ever lived. Consider Eve: *lifegiver.* The crowning jewel of all creation. The last creature to be molded by the hand of God. Eve. The helper created especially for Adam. The only woman to have known the pure, sinless love of a husband. The only woman to have known unadulterated fellowship with the Creator God, at least this side of eternity.

Consider the beauty of those two relationships. The fulfillment Eve experienced in these two pivotal relationships has become for us, her daughters, a shadowy dream, an unattainable goal.

The Scriptures don't tell us how long Eve and her husband lived in the glorious, joy-filled garden. What we do know is that within one chapter of the account of their creation, Adam and Eve disobeyed the Creator by eating fruit from the only tree that had been forbidden them. In so doing, the couple brought sin and judgment and death into the world—bringing down a curse not only on humanity but on all of creation.

According to Genesis 3, it wasn't until after the sin that Eve was named; before that, she was simply called *woman.* Soon after the infamous sin, "the mother of all the living" lived through the first eviction (of herself and her husband from the Garden God had created for them to enjoy), the first pangs of childbirth, and the first death of a son. She was the first mother to live through the grief of estrangement from one son and the death of a second. Even to this day, there is something out of order—a poignant discrepancy—when a mother outlives her child.

Consider the agony of knowing that your firstborn son had murdered his brother in a fit of rage and jealousy. Try to imagine the guilt. Could Eve have possibly been unaware that had she resisted the deception by the serpent in the Garden, sin would not have entered the world, her family would be presiding over Paradise, and both of her sons would still be alive? You can be sure she knew.

Consider the names she chose for her sons:

Cain: *possession.* "She said, 'With the help of the Lord I have brought forth a man'" (Genesis 4:1). God had allowed her to bear something of value despite her sin. There is a note of redemption here and in 1 Timothy 2:15: "But women will be saved through childbearing." Not knowing the mind of the Creator, Eve may have hoped that this would be the son who would "crush the serpent's head" (see Genesis 3:15). But Cain was not to be the man.

Abel: *breath.* Here's another irony; it was the breath of life that Cain stole from his younger brother.

Seth: *compensation, substituted.* "God has granted me another child in place of Abel, since Cain killed him" (Genesis 4:25). Through Seth's line, the promised Messiah would be traced.

In Eve's case, God allowed irony in her naming. *Lifegiver.* What an ironic name for the one whose sin, along with her husband's, brought *death* into the world. But God sees the future as if it had already happened. It's a difficult concept to grasp with our human understanding. C. S. Lewis described this concept in his *Chronicles of Narnia,* as the past, present, and future being within the Creator all at once. He isn't just all-knowing. He is all that is, all that was, all that will be; the Alpha and the Omega, the Beginning and the End (Revelation 1:8).

So God—seeing the end of all things earthly even while seeing the beginning—granted the first husband wisdom to name his wife, Eve, as a foretelling of what she would become. The forebear of Mary, who would bear the Messiah—the Messiah who would once again bring life and eternity to humanity. The One who would banish death and sin forever. The One who would redeem the race born out of Adam's and Eve's sin. The One who would once and for all bring forgiveness to even the first of all sinners, Eve.

Lifegiver. How appropriate. How wonderful. How like God.

Loving Creator, thank You that even while I was yet a sinner, You died for me. Thank You for seeing my potential, who I will be, even when I am far from achieving it. Use me to bring glory back to You, as You accomplish Your purpose in me. Amen.

11

TAMAR:
PALM TREE

> About three months later Judah was told,
> "Your daughter-in-law Tamar is guilty of
> prostitution, and as a result she is now
> pregnant." Judah said, "Bring her out and have
> her burned to death!" *(Genesis 38:24)*

Early in March, after a particularly colorless and
cold winter up north, we alighted from the airport people mover into our first sniff of fragrant
ocean air. Never had airport property looked or
smelled more appealing than to our tired party of
Chicagoans arriving in Tampa, Florida, for a late-
winter break.

After we packed our belongings into the trunk
and backseat of a rental car, we rolled down the
windows and made for the ocean. It had been
months since we had seen green leaves on trees or
colorful flowers on lawns. Yet here in this most in-
dustrial of scenes a few miles from the ocean,
people had taken the time to cultivate grassy park-
ways carpeted in patches of brilliant reds and
dotted at regular intervals with graceful green palm
trees. Welcome to Florida; won't y'all stay a while!

The palms looked so fragile, so exposed as
their branches waved in the breeze. Their oddly
leaning trunks looked timid, as though the gentle
ocean breeze could huff-and-puff them down whenever it chose. *How do these trees survive hurricane-
force winds?* Their supple makeup allows them to

bend almost in two, only to spring back up—
bruised but not broken—to face another gust. They
are pushed to the limit, but not driven past the
point that God designed them to endure.

This brings to mind God's promise to us: "No
temptation has overtaken you except such as is
common to man; but God is faithful, who will not
allow you to be tempted beyond what you are able,
but with the temptation will also make the way of
escape, that you may be able to bear it" (1 Corinthians 10:13 NKJV). We may be bent under the weight
of this world's pressures, but we need not break.

The daughter-in-law of Jacob's son Judah was
named for this remarkable tree. Tamar: *palm tree*.
Like her namesake, Tamar was pushed to the limit,
bent in two by her father-in-law's deception. But,
unlike the regal palms lining Tampa's airport ex-
pressway, Tamar did not emerge unscathed from
her temptation.

Tamar's story is filled with treachery, deceit,
and scandalous sexual sin. She was married to Er,
the eldest of Judah's three sons. But before the couple could conceive any children, "the Lord put [Er]
to death" (Genesis 38:7) because he was evil. In the
custom of the time, Judah forced his middle son
Onan to sleep with Tamar, to keep Er's name alive
by giving him an heir. Onan, however, was careful
not to conceive a child by Tamar, because he knew
the child would not be considered his. Onan's actions, too, were odious in God's sight, so God put
him to death (Genesis 38:10).

Again Judah stepped in. (You'll recall that Judah was one of the brothers who sold Joseph into
slavery; the family had a long history of deception,

and he carried on the tradition.) He'd already lost two sons, and he blamed Tamar for his losses—after all, they were both her husbands. It didn't occur to him that his own lack of integrity was more directly to blame for his sons' wickedness than anything his daughter-in-law might have done. In his grieving, illogical mind-set, Judah knew he could not bear to lose his third son, Shelah. He sent Tamar back to her parents' home to live as a widow until Shelah grew up—except, when Shelah did grow up, Judah did not fulfill his promise to give him to Tamar as her husband.

One day Tamar received word that the newly widowed Judah was going into the country to shear his sheep. So she covered her face to conceal her identity and planted herself in the path he would be traveling. "When Judah saw her, he thought she was a prostitute, for she had covered her face. Not realizing that she was his daughter-in-law, he went over to her by the roadside and said, 'Come now, let me sleep with you'" (Genesis 38:15–16a). Note that she did not entrap him; Judah approached a woman he thought was a pagan shrine prostitute and asked for sex.

Tamar agreed, for the price of a kid from Judah's flock. In lieu of the kid, she took Judah's personal signet ring and bracelets until the kid could be sent. Tamar became pregnant with twins as a result of that day's union. She did not prostitute herself again, but returned to her widow's garb. When Judah's emissary returned to retrieve the jewelry by presenting the kid, the prostitute could not be found.

When Tamar's pregnancy became known to Judah, his response was swift and heartless—he would rid himself of this scourge on his family. *Burn her at the stake!* One can imagine his self-righteous relief at having a legitimate reason to withhold his third son from her. But as she was being brought out to be killed, Tamar produced Judah's jewelry, making it clear that its owner had caused her pregnancy. "Judah recognized them and said, 'She is more righteous than I, since I wouldn't give her to my son Shelah.' And he did not sleep with her again" (Genesis 38:26). I wonder if he realized the irony that *he* was the one producing an heir for his son Er?

Tamar: used and user; deceived and deceiver. Her story is one of God's redemptive power and His mercy despite the sins of His people. Her choices cost her her good name and good standing. God didn't need her to commit this sin in order to fulfill His purpose, but He used her in spite of herself. The winds of life broke Tamar, yet God restored her to usefulness in raising the son through whose seed would come the fulfillment of His promised redemption. One of Tamar and Judah's twin boys, Perez, became an ancestor of King David, and thus a progenitor of Jesus.

God, thank You for this reminder that even when I sin, You forgive; even when my motives are wrong, You offer redemption. But the next time I am tempted, may I be like the palm tree, bent but not broken by the hurricane-force winds of evil. Amen.

12

MIRIAM:
BITTERNESS

> Then Miriam the prophetess, Aaron's sister, took a tambourine in her hand, and all the women followed her, with tambourines and dancing. Miriam sang to them: "Sing to the Lord, for he is highly exalted. The horse and its rider he has hurled into the sea." *(Exodus 15:20–21)*

For believers Sunday is the Lord's day. A day to spend worshiping Him, learning of Him, meeting with Him.

But for that to happen for the majority of the congregation, there is a team of workers for whom Sunday will not be a day of rest. My grandfather, a pastor, rose before dawn every Sunday to pray and to study his message one more time. In our household, Mom arises the earliest on Sundays; since before I was born, she has served in worship as organist and pianist.

My Sunday mornings, too, are chock-full. Take last Sunday. After a short rehearsal at home, I arrived at church. Worship team vocal practice, violin solo practice, and prayer preceded my run down the hall where I co-teach the single adult Sunday school class. While teaching, I got called away to prepare to accompany the congregation on the synthesizer (as a substitute), then I raced back to my class so my teaching partner could rush to his post as an usher. When I arrived in the sanctuary again, I had a moment before the worship team took the platform. After crisscrossing the platform a few times to the synthesizer, microphone, and violin, I sat down to hear the pastor's message—with very tired ears.

I'm neither the most talented musician nor the best vocalist. I'm at best third-string keyboard player, second-string violin, and a decent alto singer. Despite my weaknesses, God has called me to work for Him without looking at anyone else. He has called *me* to be useful to Him.

Miriam, the sister of Moses and Aaron, was called to be useful to God. Centuries after Miriam's death, the prophet Micah records God's words, "I sent Moses to lead you, also Aaron and Miriam" (6:4). So Miriam was in the upper echelon of authority—leading Israel alongside her brothers.

Her name means *bitterness*. No doubt, Jochebed and her husband, Amram, named their daughter to reflect their sorrow over their situation as slaves of the Egyptians. While Miriam started out sweetly and lived in service to God, she did need to have the root of bitterness torn out of her heart.

We first see Miriam (although here she is only identified as Moses' sister) hiding in the reeds beside the Nile to see what would happen to her baby brother, who was hidden near the bank. Pharaoh's daughter found the baby, and Miriam stepped out of the reeds. Miriam thought quickly, offering to get a Hebrew woman (the child's mother) to nurse the baby for the princess.

Years later, when God used Moses to orchestrate the release of the Hebrew slaves, his sister was beside him again. Scripture identifies her as a prophetess, one who spoke the words of God. On the banks of another body of water, the recently

parted Red Sea, Miriam led in worship to the Lord
their Deliverer. It was a beautiful praise chorus:
"Sing to the Lord, for he is highly exalted. The
horse and its rider he has hurled into the sea" (Exodus 15:21). The song overflowed from a grateful
heart. In it she recognized the awesome power of
God and called the people to do likewise.

When Miriam sang, the women took up their
tambourines and danced along behind her. *All* the
women did as she did. That was why she had to be
punished when after years of desert wandering for
the Israelites the root of bitterness came to full
bloom in Miriam's life.

Jesus said, "From everyone who has been given
much, much will be demanded" (Luke 12:48). The
leader is responsible to live an exemplary life. Not
because God capriciously holds him or her to a
higher standard, but because as does the leader, so
do the people. See it in the history of the nations of
Israel and Judah, in the books of Kings and Chronicles. When a good king ruled, the people served
the Lord; when the king served other gods, only a
remnant stayed true to the Lord.

Miriam and Aaron began to grumble against
Moses because of his marriage to a foreigner. But
soon the real issue surfaced: jealousy. The two complained: "Has the Lord spoken only through Moses?
. . . Hasn't he also spoken through us?" (Numbers
12:2).

I can imagine the conversation:

"Who does Moses think he is?" Aaron says.

"Yeah, he's nothing special," Miriam agrees.
"He's just our little brother—why, if it hadn't been

for my quick thinking, he would have died in the bulrushes."

"God uses us too," Aaron continues. "I'm the high priest; I serve in the tabernacle of God—I go into the holy of holies."

"And I'm a prophetess. Look at all those who follow me . . ."

God could not let this continue. He called the three siblings to meet Him. Sharply rebuking the pair for the presumption of speaking against His servant and the folly of trying to grab more of the ministry than He had given them, God struck Miriam with leprosy—an ugly disease that ate away first at skin, then at bone.

Moses, in humility, asked God to forgive his sister and remove this curse from her. God agreed that after seven days she could be restored. But the nation suffered for her sin—no one could move one step closer to the Promised Land until the seven days were completed. Being numbered among the grumblers, Miriam never got to see the Promised Land. She died in the desert.

Miriam had begun coveting someone else's God-given gifts. She had started focusing on how great she was. "I" and "me" showed up too often in her thoughts.

The apostle Paul begged believers, "I say to every one of you: Do not think of yourself more highly than you ought, but rather think of yourself with sober judgment, in accordance with the measure of faith God has given you" (Romans 12:3).

Rather than focusing on faithful completion of the calling God had placed on her life, Miriam wanted more—and she paid a dear price for the wanting. It would be like me trying to wrest the concert hall stage from Itzhak Perlman so I could be accompanied by a great orchestra. God has neither called nor equipped me to play the violin in a world-class symphony hall. He has called me to lead His people in worship in a medium-sized church in northwest suburban Chicagoland. That is a high calling, one for which I am grateful.

Dear Father, help me to be willing to fulfill Your calling on my life. Make me content to do no more; make me faithful to do no less. Amen.

13

MICHAL:
WHO IS LIKE GOD?

Now Saul's daughter Michal was in love
with David . . . (1 Samuel 18:20)

As the ark of the Lord was entering the City
of David, Michal daughter of Saul watched
from a window. And when she saw King David
leaping and dancing before the Lord, she de-
spised him in her heart. (2 Samuel 6:16)

Last year I picked out my first new car. In the
past, I had purchased used cars. But my grandmother bought my car from me and bought me a
new car.

It was a heady experience. I approached every
showroom full of gleaming paint jobs and shining
whitewalls knowing that one of these vehicles
could soon be mine. I did my homework, surfing
the Internet for information on dependability of
various makes within our price range. I made my
choice, paying particular attention to the color—
silver that shimmers with a hint of violet in the
sunlight. I remember most clearly the moment after
we signed the papers, when at last I drove out of
the lot in my fresh-smelling car, Grandma riding
shotgun beside me.

A week later, a friend rode beside me on our
way out to lunch. She proudly informed me that
she had just mailed the last payment on her car—
and told me that she felt it was time for a new car (a
new set of payments). At only four years old, her

car was showing signs of aging. And so would mine.

On the day my car reached its four thousandth mile, I was in an accident. I was injured, and so was my car. It was another reminder of the rule of this earth. Everything is in a state of decay. Possessions will be destroyed. My car eventually will rust (although I have a promise from the manufacturer that it will not do so for at least seven years).

No thing on this earth will remain the same.

No one on earth will remain the same, either. People will rush headlong into my life only to high-tail it back out again. King David learned this lesson in a tragic way with his first wife, Michal.

Her name meant *who is like God?* But Michal was not like God. God is unchanging. He is the same yesterday, today, and forever (Hebrews 13:8). Michal was fickle. As her emotions were swept along by the winds, so her love for her husband blew fiery hot one day, frozen cold the next.

She was the daughter of King Saul, given to David as wife to reward him for killing two hundred Philistine men. Saul, jealously hating David, gave Michal to him with ulterior motives. "'I will give her to him,' he thought, 'so that she may be a snare to him and so that the hand of the Philistines may be against him'" (1 Samuel 18:21).

At that time Michal was deeply in love with David. When she discovered that her father planned to kill her husband, she secretly lowered David out the window and lied to her father about how he got away. She protected her beloved, like a good wife should do—although deception need not have been part of her protection. The noble wife in

Proverbs 31 had this protective love for her husband: "Her husband has full confidence in her. . . . She brings him good, not harm, all the days of her life" (vv. 11–12).

Michal would have been wise to have remained true to these qualities throughout her life. But it was not to be.

While David was fleeing from the king, Saul gave Michal to another man as wife. After Saul was killed in battle, King David reclaimed Michal as his wife. Establishing his rule in Jerusalem, David determined to bring the Ark of the Covenant, the symbol of God's presence, to Jerusalem. It was such a joyful, worshipful occasion that the king celebrated with a parade where he offered many sacrifices to God. In gratitude, the king danced before the Lord, in the sight of his people. Michal, watching from a palace window, hated David for his display that day. And she didn't keep her feelings to herself.

> When David returned home to bless his household, Michal daughter of Saul came out to meet him and said, "How the king of Israel has distinguished himself today, disrobing in the sight of the slave girls of his servants as any vulgar fellow would!"
> David said to Michal, "It was before the Lord, who chose me rather than your father or anyone from his house when he appointed me ruler over the Lord's people Israel—I will celebrate before the Lord." (2 Samuel 6:20–21)

In our day, we might excuse Michal's actions, blaming them on her dysfunctional father and his use of her as a pawn against her husband. But God held Michal responsible for her sin of despising

David for his heartfelt worship. He struck her with what was considered a great curse in the Hebrew culture: "Michal daughter of Saul had no children to the day of her death" (2 Samuel 6:23).

Who, indeed, is like God? Only He is forever constant. No one and nothing on this earth can claim to be unchanging. We will age. Our bodies will deteriorate. Our tastes will change. But our love need not grow cold, as Michal's did. If we keep our hearts loyally focused on God, as David did, even when we fall short of God's expectations, we can continue to grow in our love for Him. That is a change worth pursuing.

Loving God, keep my heart from despising another in his expression of worship to You. May I instead grow in my love for others and for You. Amen.

14

VASHTI:
BEAUTIFUL

> But when the attendants delivered the king's command, Queen Vashti refused to come. Then the king became furious and burned with anger. (*Esther 1:12*)

Anyone who saw JoyAnn would immediately recognize her stunning beauty, her self-assured carriage, her sparkling smile.

When a modeling agency came to her all-girls' high school to find a fresh face, they discovered her immediately. Soon her image was gracing print ads, runways, and TV screens. They gave her lovely garments to wear: flowing gowns, dignified professional suits, playful dresses.

She had an unspoiled beauty, a genuine spirit, a naïveté. Unlike most models, JoyAnn had a beauty that went deeper than her face, deeper than her perfect figure.

Decades later, her figure has shifted a bit and a few crinkles have found their way onto that perfect face. Yet JoyAnn is still beautiful, because underlying everything visible, JoyAnn is one who loves Jesus with all her heart, one who loves others as He does. She has the brand of beauty that Peter talked about in his epistle: "Your beauty should not come from outward adornment, such as braided hair and the wearing of gold jewelry and fine clothes. Instead, it should be that of your inner self, the unfading beauty of a gentle and quiet spirit, which is of great worth in God's sight" (1 Peter 3:3–4).

King Xerxes had chosen Vashti to be his queen because of her unmistakable beauty. Even her name meant *beautiful*. So proud was he of her outward appearance that at a season of great celebration in his kingdom he wanted to show her off. In the presence of a great gathering of drunken men, the king called for Vashti to come and parade around his party wearing her royal crown. He wanted all his officials and all the men under his rule to be envious of the superior beauty of his wife to any other woman in the kingdom. It was a pride thing with Xerxes.

It was improper in the Persian culture for women and men to be entertained together. While Xerxes was throwing his extravagant seven-day banquet in the royal garden, Vashti was modestly hosting the women in her own apartment. Xerxes's command to Vashti was not in good taste. But the queen answered her husband's request with a public refusal, and in so doing she dishonored him in the eyes of his fellow revelers. His anger burned against her, and when his advisers suggested that she never again be allowed into his presence, he issued an unchangeable decree to that effect—one that he regretted later, when the alcohol wore off and his anger cooled down.

Note the words of an earlier, wiser king, Solomon: "A gentle answer turns away wrath, but a harsh word stirs up anger" (Proverbs 15:1). Although the king's request offended Vashti's dignity and sense of decorum, it was her answer that got her in trouble. Her response probably wasn't gentle.

When I was learning to drive, my father reminded me that it is possible to be technically in the right—to have the right-of-way—and yet to be involved in an accident because another driver sees things differently. My dad called it being "dead right."

Vashti was "dead right." The king's drunken command was not proper, but apparently neither was it vile. From our perspective, Vashti seems to have been well within her rights to refuse, yet doing so cost her her royal crown, her dignity, and her position. Unfortunately, we are unable to ask her, "Was it worth it?" so we can only guess at her answer. Whether or not it was worth it, the price was steep.

We could debate how a woman with a spirit of inner beauty would have responded. But as believers in Christ, we have scriptural admonitions to have the same attitude in ourselves that was in Jesus (Philippians 2:5). What was that attitude? "He humbled himself and became obedient to death" (v. 8).

Vashti's indignity doesn't even cast a slight shadow on the unspeakable indignities Jesus bore humbly, without a word. Most of the injustices we confront are more like those Vashti faced than those our Master endured for us. And yet Scriptures tell us: "Your attitude should be the kind that was shown us by Jesus Christ, who, though he was God, did not demand and cling to his rights as God, but laid aside his mighty power and glory, taking the disguise of a slave and becoming like men. And he humbled himself even further, going so far as actually to die a criminal's death on a cross" (Philippians 2:5–8 TLB).

It's a tall order for fallen humans to have the same attitude as Jesus. But in His strength those who are cloaked by God's love can demonstrate His attitude of humility and shine with His inner beauty every day of our lives.

Jesus—clothe me in Your beauty today. May my life be a shining reflection of You that will lead others to find forgiveness and love at the foot of Your Cross. Amen.

15

SARAI/SARAH:
PRINCESS/NOBLEWOMAN

Is anything too hard for the Lord? I will
return to you at the appointed time next year
and Sarah will have a son. (*Genesis 18:14*)

Every little girl longs for her daddy to tousle her
hair and call her princess. Little girls adore
those fairy tales where the scrub-slave Cinderella is
elevated to the post of princess by the love of a
charming prince, or where Snow White is awak-
ened from her bewitched slumber by the delicate
kiss of a handsome prince.

For most of us, the office of princess is not
even a vague possibility. But for the few who marry
into royal families, countless women in every country of the world live vicariously through their
charmed lives.

Consider the spectacle of the royal wedding
between Lady Diana and Prince Charles. The festiv-
ities, the processions, the galas were carried live on
international television. Who could erase from
memory the sight of the bedecked white bridal
carriage in which sat the soon-to-be-princess de-
murely clothed in dazzling white and priceless
jewels? It was every girl's dream. When Princess Diana bore her two sons, the older of whom should
someday elevate her to the role of queen mother,
her life seemed complete.

Then the fairy tale crumbled and daily life became unbearable for the fated royal pair. Soon the public's taste for the "inside scoop" could scarcely be sated. Every sordid detail was plastered across tabloids and gossip columns the world over. The princess's untimely death caused the BBC to preempt all programming to wave the flag and play the national anthem. People feasted on their pain.

Royal life, at least outside fairy tales, seldom lives up to "happily ever after." Most of us find that a sorry discovery. It's a tragedy to watch a dream crumble.

One Bible princess had to watch her dreams crumble before she would stand back and experience God's fulfillment of His promise. She started out in life as Sarai, *princess*. A very beautiful woman, she became wife to a wealthy man who was ten years older, Abram. She obediently followed her husband on his God-sent journey into a land of promise. She became Princess Sarai, mistress of the camp. We think of a princess as one who carries herself with dignity and purity, one who has probably been pampered and sheltered. This princess lived in tents in submission to her husband.

When Princess Sarai heard the Lord's promise to Abram that out of him God would make a great nation (Genesis 12:2–3), she surmised that she would be the queen mother. But as the years wore on, she bore no children.

I can hear her thinking, *He's chosen, but what about me? Maybe God plans to fulfill the promise through a younger woman who can give him a child. I have to do something.*

So, like a good royal woman, she took control

of the situation, telling her husband, "The Lord has kept me from having children. Go, sleep with my maidservant; perhaps I can build a family through her" (Genesis 16:2). So she gave her servant Hagar to Abram. Hagar quickly became pregnant and began to hate Sarai. Complaining to her husband, Sarai got the OK to do what she would with Hagar. Rather than demonstrating godly grace, she chose to mistreat the servant so severely that Hagar ran away. Even when Hagar and her son Ishmael returned, they were a constant reminder to Sarai of her barrenness. Their very presence mocked her womanhood. And Sarai hated that Abram loved the son of her servant.

Then God appeared to Abram again, to renew His covenant and to rename the couple: Abram became Abraham *(father of a multitude);* Sarai became Sarah—from *princess* she became *noblewoman.* The Lord made it clear that the son of the slave was not the child He had promised Abraham; the ninety-year-old *noblewoman* Sarah would bear the promised son. Thinking this absolutely ludicrous, first Abraham then Sarah laughed.

Despite her disbelief, God fulfilled His promise. One year later, at the appointed time (Genesis 18:14), Sarah brought her son, Isaac: *laughter,* into the world. Some quick arithmetic will show that God gave Sarah three months to wallow in her laughter of doubt before the child was conceived. As Matthew Henry notes in his commentary on this Bible passage, "Human improbability often sets up in contradiction to the divine promise. The objections of sense are very apt to stumble and puzzle the weak faith even of true believers."[1]

Sarah proved herself to be true nobility, despite her moments of doubt. She learned what it meant to be God's woman, used in His plan. Her son did become the father of the nation of Israel, although she died when he was thirty-seven and didn't even see him married. In the New Testament, the apostle Peter commends Sarah to women of his day as an example of submission to her husband (1 Peter 3:5–6). Most important, Sarah learned through the pain of poor choices that her futile attempts to control her situations could cause nothing but heartache. She learned that even when it seems humanly impossible, God will be faithful to fulfill His promise —in His way—in His time.

These are lessons modern-day princesses, noblewomen, and commoners must all learn—either vicariously from Sarah's example or from the tragedy of our own stubborn mistakes. I hope I choose the former.

God, help me to submit to Your Lordship and take You at Your Word. May I never interfere or become impatient with Your plan, no matter how long it takes before You fulfill Your promises. Amen.

NOTE
1. Genesis 18:9–15 page 5 from Matthew Henry's Commentary on the Whole Bible: New Modern Edition database © 1991, 1994 by Hendrickson Publishers, Inc.

16

HAGAR:
FLIGHT

So Hagar bore Abram a son, and Abram gave the name Ishmael to the son she had borne. (*Genesis 16:15*)

On my corkboard at work, just above my telephone, hangs a brightly colored advertising button. Like "I Like Ike" and "Vote Nixon" a generation or two ago, this button carries a powerful lesson. It's a needed admonition to me.

In bright, red letters it announces it is a 'Tude-ometer, a not-so-subtle advertisement for Patsy Clairmont's funny-but-potent book, *Sportin' a 'Tude*. The button has a spinner-style dial that measures the bearer's attitude. A person adjusts the dial to fit his current attitude (unfortunately—or maybe fortunately—it does not automatically adjust to your 'tude as the 1970s mood rings purported to do). The continuum goes from "Beatitude" all the way to the walk-ten-miles-out-of-your-way-to-avoid-me "Feud 'Tude."

It's humbling to see how often my inner dial (if not the one on the wall) is closer to Feud than Beatitude. I look up at the button when an irate caller is on the line or when a superior makes an unreasonable demand or when a coworker says something that's just plain hurtful. Life can be unfair, injustice does happen, but my attitude is always my responsibility to control with God's help.

Have you ever looked through the Bible to see how many characters—both heroes and villains—were carrying the burden of a terrible 'tude? There are more than a few. Sarah's servant Hagar had a major 'tude, one that rubbed off on all those around her (including her mistress and, most tragically, her young son)—and it took God to lift it from her.

Her name means *flight*. Twice in her life Hagar found herself in a position of fleeing to the desert in panic and dread.

The first issue that jumps out as we read Hagar's story is that her circumstances were not under her control. Life was not fair to her, at least from a human perspective. She had served Sarai faithfully for many years, had probably heard of God's promise of a son for her mistress. When Sarai got impatient with God and gave Hagar to her husband, Abram, as a concubine, Hagar doesn't seem to have had a say in the matter. It certainly wasn't her idea. The fact that Hagar conceived and eventually bore Abram a son was also a matter not of her choosing.

Then Hagar did make a choice. The Genesis account records Sarai complaining to Abram that the now-pregnant Hagar "despises" her mistress (16:5). One wonders how Hagar communicated that emotion to her mistress.

Allowed to do as she pleased, Sarai chose to mistreat Hagar, and Hagar fled into the desert. By a desert spring the angel of the Lord[1] met the fleeing servant, telling her, "Go back to your mistress and submit to her" (16:9). He also told her she would have a son, whom she was to name Ishmael (meaning *God will hear*), and that Ishmael would "live in hostility toward all his brothers." This child was not the promised son; he would never receive the inheritance of the covenant God pledged to Abram.

So she returned and bore the child. Years later, when Sarah's son Isaac was born, Ishmael mocked the child, provoking Sarah to force Abraham to send the slave and her son back into the wilderness, this time for good.

Despairing for her son's life, Hagar is once again met by "the angel of God." He promises that of Ishmael, too, He would make a great nation. God provided for the boy, who finished growing up in the desert, married an Egyptian woman, and became an archer. Modern-day Arabs trace their descent back to Ishmael.

Years later, in the New Testament, Paul chides the Roman believers, "Who are you to judge someone else's servant? To his own master he stands or falls" (Romans 14:4). We, too, must be careful not to judge Hagar too severely, as we do not know her heart. But all indications show that her service to Sarah did not spring out of love but out of obligation alone.

Remember Jesus' response to the question posed Him regarding the greatest commandment? "'Love the Lord your God with all your heart and with all your soul and with all your mind.' This is the first and greatest commandment. And the second is like it: 'Love your neighbor as yourself.' All the Law and the Prophets hang on these two commandments" (Matthew 22:37–40). A loving servant would not allow insolence or taunting to find a foothold in her heart. She could not possibly despise and love Sarah with the same heart. Most important, a loving servant would not allow her son to taunt her mistress's child.

Although humanly we would lay the blame squarely on Hagar's shoulders, God (who alone sees the whole picture) valued Hagar so much that He personally went to encourage and commission her. He rescued Hagar and her son from certain death in the desert—not once, but twice. He did make of Ishmael a great nation—in fact, many great nations.

Yes, God's ways are mysterious, far above anything we mortals could begin to fathom. His calling to us, however, is clear. He calls us to love—not just to love our friends, but our enemies. Those who taunt us. Anger us. Frustrate our every effort at every turn.

Now, anytime I'm tempted to sulk rather than forgive, anytime I'm fuming from an injustice, one glance at the 'Tude-ometer button leads me to breathe a quick prayer. Only God can bring my heart back into the Beatitude range. He is faithful to do so, when I recognize my sin, confess it, and refuse to let anger simmer on the burner of my heart.

I wonder whether a 'Tude-ometer would have helped Hagar turn her attitude around before it cost her a comfortable home in Abraham's camp.

My Lord, too often I allow my attitude to burn furiously out of control, making a bad situation even worse. Today, I commit my attitude and emotions to You, asking that You control them so I can be a living example of one who loves others as You do. Amen.

NOTE

1. This is the term most scholars agree refers to the preincarnate Christ, who occasionally appears in the Old Testament, giving guidance to His people.

17

REBEKAH:
ENSNARER

So they called Rebekah and asked her, "Will you go with this man?" "I will go," she said. So they sent their sister Rebekah on her way, along with her nurse and Abraham's servant and his men. (*Genesis 24:58–59*)

Straight out of journalism school, I secured a job as a public relations specialist for a Chicago corporation. In many ways I felt I had sold out my journalistic ideals by joining forces with the opposition. Naively, I was convinced that although journalists nobly pursued the truth with perfect objectivity, public relations professionals booby-trapped their paths, fighting with all the resources in their arsenals to keep journalists from discovering the truth.

Part of my job was to field telephone inquiries from media representatives. I received an average of ten calls per day from local or national media professionals. Mostly, they were routine inquiries—innocuous questions, easily answered.

Then one day I received a call with a different tone. The reporter identified herself as representing a local station. She failed to mention that she was the assistant to a consumer reporter, known for his bias against any corporate or government establishment.

But her manner soon gave her away. She kept interrupting my answers to her barrage of questions without listening for the context. Feeling trapped, I took down her questions and promised to find the answers.

With my boss's help, I drafted a statement that answered all of her questions clearly and honestly. Then I called her back, reading the statement verbatim, not allowing her to interrupt. Still, when the story aired, she had chosen portions of the statement, taking them out of context, making them mean the opposite of what they actually said. My naïveté was crushed; I had been ensnared by a reporter who had started out with a preconceived notion and didn't let the facts get in her way.

I felt betrayed. And I didn't even know the woman. Imagine how Isaac must have felt: deceived, entrapped by the wife he loved—Rebekah, whose name means *ensnarer.* And so she became in later years.

Her beginning didn't foreshadow the fact that she would one day live up to (or down to) her name. The first time Rebekah was introduced, she was being selected as wife to Isaac, the son of promise whom God gave to Abraham and Sarah. Abraham's servant selected her, under divinely appointed circumstances (Genesis 24). When he requested that Rebekah leave at once on a journey that would take her to her husband-to-be, her response was sweet, innocent, and compliant: "'I will go,' she said" (Genesis 24:58).

The Scriptures say Rebekah was beautiful. Upon their first meeting, Isaac loved the wife God had given him. Yet for twenty years, this couple was unable to conceive a child. Isaac prayed for his wife, reminding God of His promise to make of him a great nation.

Finally, Rebekah became pregnant with twins. Even in her womb, the two battled. And a frightened Rebekah inquired of the Lord, "Why is this happening to me?" (Genesis 25:22). God replied that this was just the beginning of the battle. The two sons she would bear represented two different nations; the older would serve the younger.

Commendably, Rebekah took God's words to heart. She believed Him and acted accordingly. But to her discredit, she favored her younger son, Jacob (God's chosen vessel), over her older son, Esau. To his discredit, Isaac favored Esau over Jacob.

Today's psychologists would point out that parental favoritism intensifies sibling rivalry. This rivalry created rifts between husband and wife, between brother and brother.

Deception ran in Rebekah's family, as it did in Isaac's. Rebekah was sister to Laban, a deceiver of the highest order, who would soon cheat his own nephew, Jacob, out of seven years of labor. Isaac's father, Abraham, had twice told foreign kings that his wife, Sarah, was only his sister (a half-truth, as she was his half-sister). Not learning from the consequences of his father's bad choice, Isaac did the same with the king of the Philistines. He too was found out and chastised.

But it was Rebekah who pulled off a great deception of her aging, ailing husband. Wanting to help God in fulfilling His promise, Rebekah saw to it that Jacob received the blessing Isaac was to bestow on his elder son.

She equipped Jacob with delicious food (fixed just how his father liked it), his brother's clothing (for a fragrant effect), and even rough goatskin to make him hairy like his brother (to meet his blind father's touch). While Isaac was expecting Esau, the son he'd sent out hunting, Rebekah made sure he got Jacob, posing as Esau. Jacob did receive the blessing (which God had intended all along), but Rebekah never saw her beloved son again. She sent him away to her brother Laban, fearing Esau's wrath. She died before he could return home.

God made good come from Rebekah's bad choice. He did bless Jacob and make of him a nation, God's own people. But Rebekah paid a dear price. Would God not have caused His promise to be fulfilled without requiring a wife's deception? Comparing Scripture to Scripture, knowing His character, the answer has to be, "Of course!"

Listen to God's words, "As the rain and the snow come down from heaven, and do not return to it without watering the earth and making it bud and flourish, so that it yields seed for the sower and bread for the eater, so is my word that goes out from my mouth: It will not return to me empty, but will accomplish what I desire and achieve the purpose for which I sent it" (Isaiah 55:10–11).

God has a purpose for giving and fulfilling His word. "This will be for the Lord's renown" says Isaiah 55:13.

So entrapment, deceit, lies are never necessary in order for the truth to come to light. It is to God's own glory that His word be fulfilled.

Being on the ensnared side of that initial exchange with a reporter taught me a great lesson: as lies weren't necessary for Rebekah and Jacob, they aren't necessary today—ever.

My Lord, help me to remember that one of Your character qualities is Truth. May I value truthfulness as You do. Keep me from ensnaring others in lies; keep me vigilant and wise to the traps others may lay for me. This I ask that You may receive the glory. Amen.

18

LEAH:
TIRED

When the Lord saw that Leah was not loved,
he opened her womb, but Rachel was barren.
(*Genesis 29:31*)

Tired is a concept I understand. Never one with an excess of energy, I have experienced extreme fatigue at a few low points in my life. Once when I was in graduate school, I was working on campus full-time, going to school full-time, writing my thesis, and submitting freelance articles regularly to one local newspaper and three national magazines. I remember lying down on the living room floor one night with books and papers spread out in front of me, wanting to study, but instead falling asleep with my head propped against the rather sharp corner of my coffee table.

But when I visited my friend the other day, a first-time mom who had given birth with the aid of a C-section and whose seven-week-old baby was colicky, I came to a new understanding of the depths of fatigue that can plague a woman's body. I empathized with her, as much as an unmarried, non-mother could possibly empathize.

As I watched my friend care for her baby, even in her exhausted state, I began to think of an Old Testament mother, Leah, whose name means *tired*. Her name turned out to be prophetic, if my friend's experience with her one child was any indication. Leah gave birth to four sons in rapid succession. Then she gave birth to two more sons and one daughter. You bet Leah was tired!

Leah lived her life in the shadow of her younger, prettier sister Rachel. The Bible portrays Leah as rather plain, perhaps with blurry vision. I can almost picture her as a modern-day outcast, squinting at the world through Coke-bottle glasses. Leah and Rachel were the daughters of Laban, a hard and conniving man. But the sisters' real trouble began when their cousin Jacob appeared in their camp, fleeing from the wrath of his twin brother, Esau (whom he had cheated out of their father's blessing).

Jacob was enchanted by Rachel immediately. Her beauty captivated him so much that Jacob agreed to become Laban's indentured servant for seven years to buy Rachel's hand in marriage. After Jacob worked the seven years, Laban pulled a switch on the wedding night, giving Leah rather than Rachel to his nephew. Jacob the deceiver didn't recognize Laban's hoax until the next morning. He awoke with his new wife beside him—and it was Leah. He was furious. So he worked out a deal with Laban that he would finish Leah's "bridal week" (honeymoon) and then work another seven years to pay for Rachel's hand in marriage.

One of the saddest passages in all the Bible records the results: "Jacob lay with Rachel also, and he loved Rachel more than Leah" (Genesis 29:30). I can't imagine the piteous feeling of rejection and sorrow Leah must have experienced: forced upon a man who didn't want her as his wife; pushed aside after only one week with her husband, replaced by her pretty little sister.

But then God intervened: "When the Lord saw that Leah was not loved, he opened her womb, but Rachel was barren" (Genesis 29:31). Each time Leah bore a son, the Bible records her thoughts, "Surely my husband will love me now" (v. 32); "Because the Lord heard that I am not loved, he gave me this one too" (v. 33); "Now at last my husband will become attached to me" (v. 34). Finally, she reached a new understanding of God, saying as she named her fourth son, Judah (*praised*), "This time I will praise the Lord" (v. 35).

Unfortunately, though, the story did not end on this note of praise. Throughout their lives in the same camp, the two sisters kept competing for Jacob's attentions. Rachel wanted Jacob's undivided attention. Leah craved the security of her husband's loving embrace. First Rachel then Leah gave Jacob their servant girls as concubines—to bear more children for him. And when Jacob and his large family encountered his twin in the wilderness, Jacob was purposeful in how he assembled his party: "He put the maidservants and their children in front, Leah and her children next, and Rachel and Joseph in the rear" (Genesis 33:2). *Thanks a lot, husband. There's no doubt whose children you value most!*

Years later, in one final scene, Jacob gave his last instructions to his sons, recorded in Genesis 49. He made them promise to bury him in the cave of his ancestors, and he mentioned specifically that this was where he had buried Leah. Rachel had died and been buried in the wilderness. But finally it was Leah's body alone beside her husband's in burial.

Graciously, God honored Leah, although her husband never did love her as much as he loved her sister. Leah's son Judah—for whom she praised God—became the ancestor of the Messiah. God chose her son, not Rachel's Joseph (whom Jacob obviously favored), to carry on His covenant with Abraham. As if to reaffirm Leah's son's favored status in God's eyes, one of Christ's names in heaven (Revelation 5:5) is *Lion of the tribe of Judah.*

Jesus, what a comfort it is to know You honor those who are most downtrodden—tired and weak and worn. May I value others as You value me, not for their passing external beauty, but for their eternal, internal worth. Amen.

19

RACHEL:
EWE (A GOOD TRAVELER)

Now Laban had two daughters; the name of
the older was Leah, and the name of the
younger was Rachel. Leah had weak eyes, but
Rachel was lovely in form, and beautiful.
(*Genesis 29:16–17*)

If you've ever traveled through Europe, spending
three weeks touring and singing, never sleeping
in the same place two nights in a row, you'll understand Dean Beard's directive: "Each of you is limited
to two pieces of luggage. Each is to be small enough
to fit under the seat in front of you."

He went on to give the minuscule measure-
ments of an acceptable bag. The size didn't leave
any space for nonessentials. I spent weeks packing
and repacking, removing anything that would
weigh me down or that was not crucial. I made certain the garments I packed were of a wash-and-
wear variety, made of fabrics that showed few wrinkles even when stuffed in tight quarters. The dean's
wisdom was quickly evident, as we wearily carried
our own bags from bus to bed after our last concert
each night.

That trip was fourteen years ago, yet whenever
I pack for a business or pleasure trip, Dean Beard's
directive echoes in my mind. I have saved miniature plastic bottles that I refill and pack with
toiletries. I pack outfits that mix and match, and I

include only garments that go from luggage to dining room to boardroom with little special care.

Coupled with a good dose of patience (which I'm sometimes lacking), these habits make me a relatively good traveler.

Dean Beard's lesson would have been useful for at least one Bible woman. Rachel's name means *a good traveler.* She was anything but true to her name. She was unpleasant and jealous, angry and irrational, carrying altogether too much baggage in her journey through life.

Rachel was the younger of two sisters. She was the pretty one, the one used to all the attention. She was accustomed to coming in first, ahead of her sister in the beauty department, probably in every department. It was Rachel with whom the patriarch Jacob fell in love when he reached the home of his uncle Laban after fleeing from the wrath of his twin brother.

Although he worked for Laban for seven years to earn Rachel's hand in marriage, Laban pulled a switch at the last moment—tricking Jacob into marrying Leah instead. Leah. Described only as one who had "weak eyes." Not too flattering. Not the woman he loved.

So Jacob worked another seven years to earn Rachel's hand. He, of anyone, should have known the damage that sibling favoritism could wreak. Yet Jacob consistently favored Rachel, his beloved wife, over Leah, the wife who had been foisted upon him.

Rachel got a raw deal. She had to share her husband with her older sister. And she responded like a child with her arms folded in defiance: *I may*

have to accept it, but I don't have to like it. So there!
What she lacked in grace, she tried to make up for
in beauty.

But God was displeased with her attitude, so
for a time He did not allow Rachel to have children.
All the while, her sister was giving Jacob son after
son. Rachel watched in horror. Her anger brewed.

Her pride was so injured that one day she
lashed out at her husband, demanding, "Give me
children, or I'll die!" (Genesis 30:1).

Wisely and angrily, he replied, "Am I in the
place of God, who has kept you from having children?" (Genesis 30:2). Unlike Jacob, Rachel was
not sharp enough to grasp that God will do as He
pleases; it is not for mere humans to make demands of Him.

Instead of taking this chiding to heart, Rachel
cooked up a plan. Reminiscent of Sarai before her,
Rachel sought to have children by her maidservant
Bilhah, whom she gave to Jacob. Bilhah bore Jacob
two sons, and Rachel gave them names that bespoke
the ongoing competition. The first she named Dan
(*a judge*), because "God has vindicated me; he has
listened to my plea and given me a son" (Genesis
30:6). The second she named Naphtali (*my wres-
tling*), because "I have had a great struggle with my
sister, and I have won" (v. 8).

Soon Leah got into the competition, giving her
servant Zilpah to Jacob. Zilpah also bore sons for
Jacob.

Finally, after Leah had borne Jacob six sons and
one daughter, the Lord enabled Rachel to conceive
and bear a son, whom she named Joseph, saying,
"May the Lord add to me another son" (v. 24). She

wasn't satisfied with her husband's love and adoration, with the two sons of her servant, or with the infant she had just borne. She still wanted more. She couldn't have been very pleasant to be around in the home. It's a wonder Jacob still loved her.

After twenty years of service, Jacob gathered up his possessions and his family and fled from his crooked father-in-law. As another indicator of her character, Rachel stole household gods from her father before the flight. Had she been discovered, she would have been killed in the presence of her relatives. But she was deceptive enough to have hidden them well (Genesis 31:19–35).

Sometime during their return to Jacob's homeland, Rachel conceived another child. And while traveling she went into labor with Benjamin. It was a difficult birth, and immediately after she was told she had borne another son, she died. A grieving Jacob buried her on the road that led to Bethlehem and marked her grave with a great pillar.

Throughout her married life, Rachel traveled with the excess baggage of bitterness and a competitive spirit. The Lord had given her many blessings that some women never attain: a loving husband, a trusted servant, a wealthy household, and eventually a healthy son. But she was never satisfied. It was never enough.

Lord, I am ashamed to admit that I see too much of myself in Rachel's dissatisfaction with Your provision. May I be grateful for the blessings You have bestowed on me instead of looking ahead to the satisfaction of my next desire. Amen.

20

JOCHEBED:
JEHOVAH IS GLORY

> Now a man of the house of Levi married a
> Levite woman, and she became pregnant and
> gave birth to a son. When she saw that he was
> a fine child, she hid him for three months.
> (Exodus 2:1–2)

It weighs just a few ounces. It's made of gold and imprinted with the emblem of five interlocking circles. And every four years it is the most sought-after prize in all the world. An Olympic gold medal—the symbol given to the one who is the best in the world.

But the medal is just the capstone of a young life that has been consumed with one overriding passion, a young person whose body has been honed and tuned for years with that one Olympic moment always in view. Only one can be the best in each competition at each venue that year. *Oh, let it be me!* these youngsters pray.

From the majestic grandeur of the opening ceremonies to the final extinguishing of the Olympic torch, the world watches and experiences the competition vicariously. Each nation cheers loudest for its own. Each team vies to bring the glory of the gold home to its respective nation. Winning Olympic gold is more than an individual achievement; every win is a reflection upon the winner's home country.

Olympic glory, bringing honor back to one's

nation, is but one tiny aspect of the greater meaning of the concept of *glory*. Yet that definition is more easily understood in our culture than any other meaning. Among other definitions, Webster's dictionary says glory is "great beauty and splendor: magnificence" or "something marked by beauty or resplendence."

Countless times in Scripture, we are told that how we run our race ought to bring glory back to God—to bring Him praise and honor, to be worthy of His magnificence. In the Westminster Shorter Catechism, a concise synopsis of the message of the gospel, church Fathers determined that "the chief end of man is to glorify God, and to enjoy him forever."

One woman in particular fulfilled the prophetic nature of her name. Jochebed: *Jehovah Is Glory.* Her creative preservation of her younger son brought glory to God. Jochebed was the birth mother of Moses. Hers is a story of God's directing events from backstage—out of sight, out of human hearing range—of His intimately involving Himself in all that affects His people.

During the depths of the Israelites' Egyptian enslavement, Jochebed, a Levite woman, married a Levite man, Amram. They had three children: Aaron, Miriam, and Moses. Moses was born at a time when Pharaoh had decreed that midwives slaughter all Hebrew boy babies at birth. This Pharaoh didn't remember the Hebrews' ancestor Joseph, whose wise leadership had saved Egypt from starvation generations before. This Pharaoh was insecure, afraid the Israelites were being "too fruitful," multiplying too quickly.

Moses was a strong, healthy infant. Jochebed would not allow him to be killed. If a midwife didn't kill a Hebrew baby, she could be killed, as would the child. In saving Moses, Jochebed either delivered him without a midwife or put not only herself but also a midwife's life at risk.

For three months, Jochebed successfully hid the child. "But when she could hide him no longer, she got a papyrus basket for him and coated it with tar and pitch. Then she placed the child in it and put it among the reeds along the bank of the Nile. His sister stood at a distance to see what would happen to him" (Exodus 2:3–4).

What must Jochebed have been feeling as she squeezed her son for the last time, kissed his tender forehead, and brushed her index finger over his perfect little features? Where could a mother find the strength to set her child among the reeds and turn to walk away? She didn't know Pharaoh's daughter would come to that spot to bathe just as the baby was crying. She didn't know God would soften the heart of the pampered heathen girl and cause compassion to well up inside her. And she didn't know her little Miriam would emerge from the reeds and deftly offer to find a Hebrew woman to nurse the child for Pharaoh's daughter. She only knew she was abandoning her son, placing him in God's care, and possibly leaving him to die.

Imagine Jochebed's absolute, glorious joy when Miriam came running to get her: "Mommy, come quick. Pharaoh's daughter wants you to nurse the baby for her. *Our* baby! Mommy, hurry!" (OK, so they spoke Hebrew, not English. The words were different—but the sentiment is unmistakable.) In the end Pharaoh's daughter paid Moses' Hebrew mother to nurse her own son and teach him his heritage.

When Moses grew up, he became known as the son of Pharaoh's daughter. He lived in the palace and learned to be a leader by watching his adopted grandfather's example—yet another preparation for his years of leading millions of Israelites through a vast wilderness. But as a child, he frolicked in the tender arms of his loving mother, who had risked her own life to save his.

In the same way, God often uses people who live most of their days in obscurity to do His greatest works on earth. Joseph Stowell, in his book *Shepherding the Church,* tells the story of the unbroken string of evangelists from D. L. Moody to Billy Graham. One evangelist led another future evangelist to the Lord. God always raised up a man for the hour, and the chain remains unbroken. Stowell makes the point that one seemingly insignificant man started the chain: Edward Kimball, the Sunday school teacher who made a special trip to a shoe store to be sure a young man from his class, D. L. Moody, would come to know the Lord.[1]

God always has a plan that will bring glory to Himself and will achieve good for His body. Often He enlists the cooperation of seemingly insignificant people in apparently tedious circumstances to fulfill His glorious will. Such was the case with His willing servant Jochebed and with the pastor who encouraged a Sunday school teacher's concern for lost young people like D. L. Moody. Each of them ran the race of faith to win the prize—not of perishable Olympic gold but of an eternity of worshiping and basking in God's unfathomable, resplendent glory.

Lord Jesus, use me to do Your tasks—large or small. I will trust You even if You call me to a task that seems humanly impossible; for if You call, You will provide. Amen.

NOTE

1. Joseph Stowell, *Shepherding the Church* (Chicago: Moody, 1997), 94.

21

ZIPPORAH:
BIRD

Jethro, Moses' father-in-law, together with Moses' sons and wife, came to him in the desert, where he was camped near the mountain of God. Jethro had sent word to him, "I, your father-in-law Jethro, am coming to you with your wife and her two sons." *(Exodus 18:5–6)*

We have a sycamore tree in our yard, just on the back edge of our patio. My dad calls it his Zaccheus tree. Year after year, families of cardinals nest in that tree. They weave through its branches, entwining sticks, twigs, discarded yarn, paper, anything to make old Zaccheus's branches a cuddly home for their young broods.

Over the course of a spring and a summer, Dad spends hours whistling birdcalls out the screen door. He calls, they mimic. They call, he mimics. I think he succeeds in driving them a little crazy. Sometimes they'll chase his call right up to the door, where he stands safely inside.

The other day, I stopped and watched Dad's little buddies for a while. We've all noticed the swift swishes of red flash through the sky. The male cardinal seems quite sure he is as gorgeous as a peacock. But have you ever paid attention to the female? Although not as brightly colored, she has a beauty of her own. Her beauty is in the detail. Her feathers are delicately patterned, fashioned by the creative hand of God.

The mama bird is persistent, busily going

about the work of providing food for her growing brood. Back and forth she flies, bringing goodies from below to the safe haven of her nest. And don't you dare come anywhere near her brood. One year, she chose to nest on the roof just above our back door. All summer long, mama cardinal made it clear that we dare not pass through that door.

Moses' wife Zipporah (her name means *bird*) was in some ways like the mama cardinal. Her life was one of busily working to supply her family. But Zipporah's husband spent a great deal of time away from the family, busily going about God's work. So she had much of the day-to-day responsibility thrust onto her shoulders.

We meet Zipporah in Exodus 2. She was one of the daughters of Jethro (who was also called Reuel), a Midianite priest. Zipporah and her sisters were shepherding her father's flock. Moses came to the girls' aid when male shepherds tried to intimidate them. In gratitude, the priest gave Zipporah to become Moses' wife.

Their early years of marriage seem to have been fairly typical. Zipporah and Moses had two sons during that time. But when God issued His burning-bush call on Moses' life, everything changed for the couple. With his father-in-law's blessing, Moses took his family and began to return to Egypt to confront Pharaoh.

In a confusing passage, God met the family along the way and was about to kill Moses. God's anger had something to do with Moses' failure to circumcise at least one of his sons. "But Zipporah took a flint knife, cut off her son's foreskin and touched Moses' feet with it. 'Surely you are a bridegroom of blood to me,' she said. So the Lord let him alone" (Exodus 4:25–26). Thus, Zipporah proved herself a tough, obedient servant of God, who would go to great lengths to protect her husband from harm.

Moses sent his wife and sons back to Jethro soon after this incident, perhaps in an attempt to keep them from bondage in Egypt. But after Moses had led the Israelites through the Red Sea, Jethro brought Zipporah and the two boys to the desert. There is no further mention of Zipporah by name in the Scriptures. Commentators disagree as to whether she was Moses' Cushite wife mentioned in Numbers 12; she may have died before that time. (This is the episode where Miriam and Aaron sinned against Moses by their anger at his marriage to a foreign woman.)

Regardless of whether she was rejected or accepted by her husband's siblings, try to imagine the raw emotion Zipporah endured. When she married Moses, she had no reason to believe he would be anything more or less than an ordinary husband. Suddenly he started talking about meeting God at a burning bush that the fire did not consume and about setting his people free from slavery.

Then her quick action was all that stood between her husband's life and his death. After he sent her away, Zipporah doubtless missed Moses every day. Imagine her joy when her father received word of the successful Exodus God had engineered for Israel with Moses at the helm. Then, think of the little family's happy reunion in the desert.

Don't you wonder how she responded to the change in Moses, from exiled shepherd to the chief of a multimillion-member multitude? She lived out the rest of her days following her husband and a band of strangers on a circuitous wilderness trek. Living in tents. Listening to the masses complain against her husband. Seeing his face glow as he came down from his mountaintop meeting with Jehovah. Rubbing his sagging shoulders as the weight of leadership threatened to overwhelm him.

I find myself hoping she had at least one lady friend, one confidante, one soul mate who would encourage her heart, build her up, and equip her to minister to her husband during the arduous journey.

There is so much the Bible doesn't tell us about Zipporah. Yet we do catch a glimpse of the sacrifices she made for the sake of her husband's ministry. In our day, many ministry wives labor under similar circumstances. Can we build them up and encourage their hearts along the way?

God, may I be an encouragement today to someone for whom the work of ministry is becoming a heavy load. May I hold her up in prayer and make myself available as a trustworthy friend. Amen.

22

RAHAB:
PROUD

By faith the prostitute Rahab, because she welcomed the spies, was not killed with those who were disobedient. (*Hebrews 11:31*)

As reviews editor of *Moody* magazine, I traveled to annual conventions that featured up-and-comers in publishing and the music industry. Publicists wooed me with premiums and concert tickets, trying to set up opportunities for me to interview the hottest names on their lists. Their purpose was to get me to mention their products in my column.

At one convention I interviewed forty-four personalities in five days. It was a proud moment: little me hobnobbing with all these powerful thinkers, all these important performers.

As I walked the convention floor, many people in the booths glanced at my badge to determine whether I was worth their time. Then they showered me with attention, offered me free products, barely let me pass through their corridors without the promise of a review.

The next year I was promoted to a new position where I could no longer influence the reviews section. That year, I walked the same convention floor, ignored. I felt deflated. Where the previous year I had been a "somebody," now I was a "nobody." I realized that it was not I, but my position, that was sought. I was most disappointed that some of those with whom I had developed deeper friendships had no time for more than a hello now.

Pride. Those of you who think you are standing, cautioned the apostle Paul, be careful lest you fall. I was tempted to take an ego trip because of the attention I had become accustomed to receiving. Likewise, some of the exhibitors were demonstrating their own brand of pride by only paying attention to someone with the capacity to do something for them.

Yet there is a good brand of pride—one that, rather than reflecting arrogance, reflects what one dictionary calls "a sense of one's own proper dignity or value."[1] This kind of pride was demonstrated in the Scriptures by Rahab, whose name means *proud*.

Rahab ran a business in Jericho. She was known as Rahab the harlot, but she apparently had left that life of sin and become a reputable innkeeper whose establishment made up part of the city wall. Having contact with those passing through her city, Rahab had begun to hear many marvelous and fearsome stories about the God of the desert-wandering Israelites: the God who parted seas. Who conquered kingdoms and squelched all opposition. Who promised the desert wanderers eternal rights to the land on which her establishment stood.

One day a delegation of Israelite spies walked into Rahab's doorway. She knew this was the beginning of the end, so she made a deal with the spies. She would provide them safe passage out of Jericho if they promised to spare the lives of her household when they took possession of the land. The spies agreed, instructing Rahab that when the invasion began she should hang a scarlet cord in the window of her house, keeping all her family inside.

No sooner had she lowered the spies out her window and sent them into hiding, than Rahab heard a pounding on her door. The rulers of Jericho were looking for the spies. She lied about where the men had gone, giving the men the opportunity to get back to their camp without incident.

Loving her family and wanting to protect them, Rahab risked the fury of her people to protect God's representatives. Although God would not want her lying to Jericho's rulers, He did use her deception to further His agenda—to keep the spies from harm.

Rahab gathered her family and hung the scarlet cord. "So the young men who had done the spying went in and brought out Rahab, her father and mother and brothers and all who belonged to her . . . Joshua spared Rahab the prostitute . . . because she hid the men Joshua had sent as spies to Jericho—and she lives among the Israelites to this day" (Joshua 6:23, 25).

Like everyone in her day, Rahab heard the stories about the Israelites' God. But, instead of proudly hardening her heart, she humbly believed. She had a proper perspective of herself and of God —a proper pride. Listen to the faith in her words, "I know that the Lord has given this land to you" (Joshua 2:9). "The Lord your God is God in heaven above and on the earth below" (v. 11). She held in her heart the assurance that God would fulfill His promise by giving His people the land of Canaan.

Many Israelites had shown less faith than this Canaanite former prostitute.

Rahab, the woman with a realistic view of herself and of God, was commended in the New Testament both for her works (James 2:25) and for her faith (Hebrews 11:31). According to Rabbinical tradition she is an ancestor of several Israelite prophets, including Jeremiah and Huldah. More important, Rahab is one of four women Matthew mentions specifically in the lineage of Jesus. A former prostitute as a distant mother to the promised Messiah—yet another assurance that although Jesus was fully God, He was also fully human. To have been in the line of the Messiah was a great honor to which Rahab certainly never aspired. Yet God was aware of her heart's great faith.

When God looks over my life, will He find me with an arrogant pride over all of the things I have accomplished for Him, or will He find me with a humble, faith-filled spirit of praise for the many tasks He has entrusted to me? It's my choice. And it's yours.

God, plant in me a faith like the one that lived in Rahab. May I maintain an accurate view of who I am in light of who You are. Amen.

NOTE

1. *American Heritage Dictionary,* 3d ed., s.v. "pride."

23

DEBORAH:
BEE

> Deborah, a prophetess, the wife of Lappidoth,
> was leading Israel at that time. She held court
> under the Palm of Deborah between Ramah
> and Bethel in the hill country of Ephraim, and
> the Israelites came to her to have their disputes
> decided. (*Judges 4:4–5*)

I still have nightmares about it.

My company sent me to several training sessions to equip me to handle corporate public relations in crisis situations. Some of the training drills were held in an emergency command center, an electronic beehive. If you've ever seen a horror picture on video or in a theater, you have some context. It was like being in the nerve center of an electronic beast that had just initiated a self-destruct sequence.

Emergency beacons from terminals and control boards around the room reflected intermittent red lights on my computer screen. Alarms and beeps pierced the air. As one was silenced, a second sounded catastrophe on yet another front.

Trainees under the unmistakable influence of adrenaline rushed around in fast-forward mode. Pushing buttons. Holding hush-hush conferences. Feeding me technical information that was to be translated and written up for presentation at semi-hourly mock news conferences. When the computers went down, I had to handwrite the press releases. Finally, someone located a manual typewriter. Hour after hour it persisted. The keys clicked more quickly than I knew my fingers could move.

Appetites ceased, replaced by an awful gut-burning feeling. Tums and Rolaids were consumed by the carton. Finally, after eight hours, the all-clear sounded, and the drill was over. I remember sinking into my plastic workstation chair feeling as drained as if I had just lived through a real emergency.

And it was only a drill.

I can't begin to imagine how it would have felt to be Deborah, the judge of Israel during the emergency of a country being dominated by the spirit-crushing subjection to a Canaanite king. Aptly named, Deborah *(bee)* was God's woman for a crisis time. God raised her up to be a "mother" for His people. They were beaten down as a result of their disobedience and their failure to remain true to their God in the Promised Land. But God in His mercy brought this woman onto the scene, a woman who distinguished herself for her humility, wisdom, and willingness to serve.

Although she lived in a cruel, heartless time, Deborah was busy about the Lord's work. She held court under a palm tree. She listened to the people carefully and judged them in fairness and justice. She settled their arguments. She was wife of Lappidoth, yet she led God's people, as well as taking care of a household. There is no indication that her home suffered for lack of care while she was engaged in God's work. She had to have been "busy as a bee." I picture her as the Queen Bee, overseeing the activity of her hive—her nation.

In all this activity, Deborah found time to listen for God's voice. When, over the course of years, she had proven faithful in this important calling, God called her to an even greater mission: deliverance of His people from Canaanite subjection.

At God's direction Deborah called for Barak, a man from Kedesh, many miles to the north of the hill country that served as her headquarters. Barak came at her request, and Deborah passed on to him God's battle plan. She was careful to preface the plan with a justification: he was to do this not because Deborah said so, but because "the Lord, the God of Israel, commands you" (Judges 4:6).

Barak listened and agreed to go—but only on one condition. "If you go with me, I will go; but if you don't go with me, I won't go." This was quite an endorsement of Deborah's leadership ability and the veneration she had earned from God's people. Even a warrior, a man of supposed valor, knew God was with Deborah, and he wouldn't proceed without having her fighting beside him.

Yet this stipulation displeased God, and thus His servant Deborah. She agreed to go with Barak into battle, but she let him know that because of this disobedient request, he would not receive the honor for killing the Canaanite commander Sisera —that honor would go to a woman. Obediently, Barak led the warriors into battle at the command and encouragement of Deborah.

The Lord fought on Israel's behalf. It was not military might that impressed God and caused Him to act on His people's behalf. Nor did He need the scheming wisdom of men. All He required was a willing servant who listened and did His will. God gave them victory and handed Sisera over to a woman named Jael (*mountain goat*), who drove a tent peg through his temple.

After achieving the victory, Deborah was quick to lead Barak and all of Israel in a victory song that retold the story of Israel's backsliding and of the victorious battle. Throughout the song, Deborah gave all the glory to the Lord—leading the people to do the same. The result was forty years of peace for the Israelites, until they once again fell away to serve other gods.

While Deborah was busy about the urgent work of God, she listened for the important. She lived as one who graciously helped others to do God's will. She equipped the people to serve God with honesty and justice; she equipped Barak to do what he would not have done otherwise—fight for his people's freedom. And she taught the people by example that the glory goes to God alone.

My Lord, may I be as useful to You as was Your servant Deborah. May I listen for Your voice and act on Your direction, seeking only Your glory and not my own. Amen.

24

NAOMI/MARA:
MY DELIGHT/BITTERNESS

> I went away full, but the Lord has brought
> me back empty. Why call me Naomi? The Lord
> has afflicted me; the Almighty has brought
> misfortune upon me. (*Ruth 1:21*)

Christy is a sophomore in college. The newness of her freshman year is gone, but she's not an upperclassman yet. She's caught in limbo. She spent last summer in her parents' home, working several jobs and writing a column for a teen magazine. She dreamed constantly of the life and friends she had left behind—wishing she could "go home" to campus again.

Once during the summer, Christy visited campus, several hundred miles from her parents' home outside St. Louis. Campus felt odd, deserted; she saw only one person she knew. Not even her professors were there.

St. Louis continued to feel odd to her, as well. Her belongings were piled in boxes on the floor of her childhood bedroom. She didn't unpack, because she would be leaving soon. She was most at home in the netherworld of cyberspace, where she communicated via e-mail with friends scattered across the country.

Once fall came, Christy packed up and returned to campus, only to find that things had changed there too. She confided the other day that she just wanted to go home—but that she isn't quite sure where home is. It's all so confusing.

Christy may be able to relate to one Bible woman: Naomi. Her name means *my delight,* but at one point Naomi was feeling so undelightful that she asked to be called Mara (*bitterness*) instead. Christy would relate because Naomi, too, was displaced from her home.

Naomi was an Israelite, born and raised in the Promised Land—the land where God promised to care for His people, as long as they served only Him. When famine hit the Promised Land, Naomi's husband uprooted his wife and two sons, leaving his country for the alien land of Moab, whose inhabitants served grotesque foreign gods.

God did not abandon His people; He provided for those in Israel during the famine. Soon, years of prosperity returned. Yet Naomi's family remained in Moab. I can almost hear her voice in Thomas Moore's nineteenth century poem "As Slow Our Ship."[1]

> *So loath we part from all we love,*
> *From all the links that bind us:*
> *So turn our hearts, as on we rove,*
> *To those we've left behind us!*

Naomi's sons reached marrying age in Moab and took Moabite wives—another departure from God's explicit commands. (Israelites were not to intermarry with idol-worshiping foreigners.) Soon Naomi's husband and her sons died, leaving three childless widows. In her grief, Naomi's longing for home intensified. Knowing she could never receive God's blessing or be covered by His covenant while she was outside the protection of His will, she determined to journey home to the Promised Land.

Her daughters-in-law, loving Naomi, determined to journey to Israel with her. When she was not grieving, she must have been true to her name: a delight to be near. But in her depression and sorrow, Naomi begged them to stay in their own land, return to their own gods, and let her return to her homeland empty.

Naomi knew too well the persistent tug of home on the heart of a displaced person. She wanted to spare these two women whom she loved that desperate pain of always looking back toward those left behind. That she urged Ruth and Orpah to stay in their familiar surroundings makes good sense from one angle. But it is difficult to comprehend why Naomi encouraged them to stay knowing she was sending them away from Jehovah and back to pagan gods.

At Naomi's insistence, Orpah reluctantly and tearfully chose to return to her parents' home. Ruth, perhaps more stubborn, continued on with Naomi. Ruth had come to know Jehovah, through her friend Naomi, and she wasn't about to leave either of them.

It would be easy for us, with the cushion of millennia of distance from Naomi's pain, to judge her for allowing her judgment to be clouded by depression. Yet most of us have experienced sorrow and can empathize with her deep emotional upheaval. In fact, recognizing the difficulty of decision making at this time, most grief counselors advise that a widow not make any major life decisions in the first year after her husband dies.

When Ruth and Naomi arrived in Israel, Naomi's old friends greeted them happily, rejoicing to see her—another evidence that she had been a delightful friend. Still in her depressed state, Naomi begged them to call her Mara—to share her grief.

Then God proved Himself faithful; He made good on His promises by providing for the widows through the persistent work of Ruth. Recognizing God's hand in the provision, Naomi began to emerge from the depths. When her clouded thinking cleared, she began making plans for the care of her daughter-in-law. Proving her loyalty, love, and friendship, Naomi began thinking of Ruth's good, rather than her own.

God stepped in again, providing Ruth with a loving husband and an infant son. Again, Naomi's neighbors rejoiced with her: "The women said to Naomi: 'Praise be to the Lord, who this day has not left you without a kinsman-redeemer. May he become famous throughout Israel! He will renew your life and sustain you in your old age. For your daughter-in-law, who loves you and who is better to you than seven sons, has given him birth'" (Ruth 4:14–15).

Naomi had finally come home. And some day, Naomi, Ruth, Christy, each of us who serve the Living God, will reach that forever-home we're longing for, the home with streets of gold where our forever-Friend will welcome us—our heavenly home where Jesus will be our eternal Husband.

Lord, keep alive in me the longing for the eternal home You are preparing for me. In the meantime, keep me protected in the center of Your will. Amen.

NOTE

1. This is part of the first stanza of *As Slow Our Ship* by Thomas Moore. Quoted from *The Library of World Poetry* (New York: J. B. Ford, 1970).

25

ORPAH:
GAZELLE

> Then Naomi said to her two daughters-in-law, "Go back, each of you, to your mother's home. May the Lord show kindness to you, as you have shown to your dead and to me."
> (Ruth 1:8)

> *FAREWELL! if ever fondest prayer*
>   *For other's weal availed on high,*
> *Mine will not all be lost in air,*
>   *But waft thy name beyond the sky.*
> *'T were vain to speak, to weep, to sigh:*
>   *Oh! more than tears of blood can tell,*
> *When wrung from guilt's expiring eye,*
>   *Are in that word—Farewell!—Farewell!*[1]

When we embark on a journey—perhaps as a young student leaving home for the first time to trot off to college—we think only of the excitement and adventure ahead. Too often, we give not a second thought to the ones left behind, forgetting entirely those who have to rebuild a day-to-day life devoid of our presence.

This poem penned by the British poet Lord Byron in the early nineteenth century expresses the sentiment of countless thousands of friends and lovers who, down through the ages, have bid their loved ones a heart-wrenching, tear-filled farewell.

Such is the case with Naomi's daughter-in-law Orpah. Her life story dropped out of Scripture the moment she decided to heed Naomi's pleading to stay with her own people. Let's examine what

Scripture tells us of Orpah, to help us understand
(rather than judge) the response of this grieving
young widow.

Her name means *gazelle*. But did she speed
away from Naomi and Ruth like a gazelle? Did she
leap at the chance for freedom? Did she bound onto
the heights of her new adventure of returning home
to find a new husband? Not at all.

Orpah was one of three widows in the family.
Naomi's husband had died first. Then her two sons
(one married to Orpah, the other to Ruth) each
died, leaving no heirs in the family. The three
women clung together for support. Drying each
other's tears, while shedding their own. Imagine the
deep grieving in that household.

When the widowed Naomi decided to return
to her ancestors' land of Judah, Orpah and Ruth
joined her on the journey (Ruth 1:7). But Naomi
pled with them: "Go back, each of you, to your
mother's home. May the Lord show kindness to
you, as you have shown to your dead and to me.
May the Lord grant that each of you will find rest in
the home of another husband" (vv. 8–9).

Did you catch that phrase in the middle: not
only Ruth, but also Orpah, had shown kindness to
her husband and to her mother-in-law. I envision
Orpah as having the characteristics of her namesake: graceful and delicate—perhaps petite (a
gazelle stands only two feet high)—with soft, ex-
pressive eyes. When Naomi tried to send her away,
Orpah clung to her beloved mother-in-law. Her
doe-eyes were rimmed red from tears. She wondered if she'd ever have them dry again. She
couldn't imagine a life apart from this woman who

had cared for her, for whom she had cared. *No, I won't leave you,* her heart cried. Her voice cracked as she and Ruth promised, "We will go back with you to your people" (Ruth 1:10).

But Naomi insisted. And Orpah listened intently. *She does have a point. Naomi has no more sons to marry. I would be a foreigner and an alien in a land where my people have been hated for generations. Naomi has no source of income, not even a home to return to. She'll be depending on the kindness of distant relatives. Surely, those relatives will welcome my beloved Naomi home, but what about me? Just as surely, they would not welcome a penniless Moabite.*

Orpah's better judgment won out over her emotion. So amid more tears, she kissed Naomi good-bye and returned to her people—and to her gods (1:15), according to Naomi.

What were the Moabite gods like? Well, one in particular was Chemosh. Inhabitants of Moab's cities were known to have sacrificed humans to appease the wrath of Chemosh.

Wallowing in her own grief, Naomi failed to consider that in encouraging her daughters-in-law to return to their people, she was sending them back into bondage to unthinkably cruel gods. Why would Orpah return to serving a capricious god like this in exchange for placing her allegiance in the demanding but loving God of the Israelites? Would the comfort she received from her countrymen make up for the eternal loss of a relationship with the God of All Comfort?

The tragedy is not that Orpah stayed behind. We can all see the wisdom in not embarking on that journey apart from God's sovereign direction. But if

Naomi's statement was accurate—if Orpah returned to her gods—that's a sad end to one who had been exposed to day-to-day life in a household that served the true God of the universe.

Perhaps the next time we are tempted to take the logical road rather than the one that leads to the heart of God, we will remember the calamity of Orpah. She was so close to being a part of God's miraculous provision that Ruth and Naomi were soon to experience, yet in fear and sorrow, Orpah turned away. Therein is the tragedy.

> *Oh! more than tears of blood can tell,*
> *When wrung from guilt's expiring eye,*
> *Are in that word—Farewell!—Farewell!*[2]

Farewell, young Orpah. A sad farewell to the one who chose to be left behind.

Awesome God, let me not be led away from You by any human logic or reason. Let the wisdom and counsel I seek come only from You. Keep me from choosing to serve any god but You alone. Amen.

NOTE

1. This is the first stanza of *Farewell! If Ever Fondest Prayer* by Lord George Gordon Byron. Quoted from *The Library of World Poetry* (New York: J. B. Ford, 1970).

2. Ibid.

26

RUTH:
FRIENDSHIP

> May the Lord repay you for what you have
> done. May you be richly rewarded by the Lord,
> the God of Israel, under whose wings you have
> come to take refuge. (*Ruth 2:12*)

Nancy and Jan led a women's Bible study together. In fact, they did nearly everything together.

Having started in a home with a few women
learning the Scriptures together, the study group
quickly outgrew that modest dwelling and was re-
located to a mansion. Nancy and Jan had something special; together they sought the Scriptures in
preparation for leading others to do the same. God
clearly was blessing this ministry of two godly
women.

My memories of the group were limited to the
days when school was not in session. My mom
would be seated at the piano accompanying the
chorus time. At least she had a seat. I remember
women *everywhere*. Sitting on folding chairs. Lining
the living room floor. Seated at the dining room
table. Seated *under* the dining room table. Perched
all the way up the staircase.

I was there the day a tearful Jan announced
that her husband had been transferred out of state
and that she would be moving away. Nancy's response has stayed with me. She told the saddened
group, "In life, we have *maybe* one heart-to-heart

friend, one kindred spirit with whom we can share every part of our lives. Jan has been that for me. It will be different for us with miles between us. Our friendship can't help but change. But no one could ever replace the kind of friendship God has given us. There will never be another friend like Jan."

Mention that true, deep, abiding friendship in the context of Scripture, and a few pairs come to mind. The two most famous are David and Jonathan, Ruth and Naomi. Let's focus our attention on the second pair—on the friendship Ruth offered to Naomi.

Ruth the Moabitess. Even her name means *friendship*.

You've read about the circumstances that brought Ruth and Naomi together. Two widows. Mother-in-law and daughter-in-law. Naomi was a long way from home, in the land of her people's enemies. Ruth was a daughter of that land, but had proven herself to be a loving wife to Naomi's son and now a loving daughter to Naomi.

In her love and loyalty, Ruth refused to be persuaded to let Naomi make the journey back to Israel on her own. Forsaking her own people to become one of Naomi's, forsaking her own gods to serve the true God, Ruth proclaimed her allegiance. There is a poetic aura to Ruth's words, especially in King James English: "Intreat me not to leave thee, or to return from following after thee: for whither thou goest, I will go; and where thou lodgest, I will lodge: thy people shall be my people, and thy God my God: Where thou diest, will I die, and there will I be buried: the Lord do so to me, and more also, if ought but death part thee and me" (Ruth 1:16–17 KJV).

Ruth's love for Naomi was pure, seeking the best for the beloved one ahead of the best for one's self. At the time, Naomi was not in a lovable mood. She was sullen, depressed, beaten down. When the pair reached Naomi's hometown, Naomi told her friends to call her Mara (*bitter*). Meanwhile, Ruth sought a way to care for the needs of her mother-in-law.

She went out behind the barley harvesters to glean whatever they had left behind. She took the scraps, the leftovers, and ground them into food for Naomi and for herself. She so distinguished herself that when Boaz, the owner of the fields, inquired about her, his foreman told of her loyalty to Naomi and of her steady, persistent work. Boaz told Ruth, "I've been told all about what you have done for your mother-in-law since the death of your husband—how you left your father and mother and your homeland and came to live with a people you did not know before. . . . May you be richly rewarded by the Lord, the God of Israel, under whose wings you have come to take refuge" (Ruth 2:11–12). Later he told her, "All my fellow townsmen know that you are a woman of noble character" (3:11).

Boaz fed Ruth from his own table. Unselfishly, Ruth ate some but kept the rest aside to take home to Naomi that evening. God rewarded Ruth's unselfish labor by leading her to the fields of Naomi's relative Boaz and allowing her to find favor with him and glean behind his reapers throughout the barley and wheat harvests.

This knowledge brought cheer to Naomi. Soon, Naomi began to think of Ruth's safety and of

providing for Ruth's future. Unselfishness begat unselfishness.

Naomi instructed Ruth in some customs of the
time. It was time for Ruth to find a new husband.
Naomi told her to go during the night and lie down
at the foot of Boaz's bed to request that he marry
her, because he was a relative of their husbands.
Much of the meaning of that custom is lost on us; it
must have sounded odd to the foreigner Ruth, as
well. But she told Naomi, "I will do whatever you
say" (Ruth 3:5).

Through a few more twists of plot, Boaz married Ruth. Together they had a son, Obed. When
Obed grew up, he had a son: Jesse. Jesse became
the father of King David. So Ruth the Moabitess became the great-grandmother of the greatest king
Israel ever had. Furthermore, Ruth is one of the
four women mentioned in Matthew's genealogy of
Jesus Christ (1:5). Not Sarah. Not Rebekah. Not
Leah. Just Tamar, Rahab, Bathsheba, and Ruth.

Ruth shared God's blessing with her friend
Naomi. The scriptural account notes, "Naomi took
the child, laid him in her lap and cared for him.
The women living there said, 'Naomi has a son'"
(Ruth 4:16–17). Ruth had worked hard and over-
come many obstacles to prove her loyal friendship.
In so doing, she unknowingly proved herself wor-
thy of her future kinship with royalty.

*Lord, in the past I have prayed that I might find the
kind of friend who would be my kindred spirit. Today,
instead, I pray that I may be the kind of friend that
Ruth was to Naomi: faithful, trustworthy, loving, and
generous. Amen.*

27

BATHSHEBA:
DAUGHTER OF AN OATH

> One evening David got up from his bed and
> walked around on the roof of the palace. From
> the roof he saw a woman bathing. The woman
> was very beautiful, and David sent someone to
> find out about her. The man said, "Isn't this
> Bathsheba, the daughter of Eliam and the wife
> of Uriah the Hittite?" (2 Samuel 11:2–3)

S he's amazing." "So together." "Always in control." "Self-assured."

I've overheard all of these descriptions of my
lifelong best friend. The person she'd have you see
is as near to perfection as any woman can be in this
life. I'm not saying that she isn't amazing, put together, and self-assured. In fact, in my life, she
often has been very much like Mary Poppins:
"Practically perfect in every way." It's just a dangerous thing to assume others' public faces portray
their private selves.

The other day, I found her close to tears. I invited her into my home office for a round of computer games. Sometimes, in those frivolous times,
we can solve the world's problems together—and if
not the world's problems, certainly our own.

That night, our conversation was more of a
monologue. She spoke; mostly, I listened.

She tried to process how her motives could
have been so misunderstood. She had asked someone to collaborate in a project with her, anticipating
that the other person would share her excitement at

the potential partnership. Instead, she received a verbal lashing for not having asked sooner.

As a tear splashed into her coffee mug, I couldn't help wondering how shocked those who see only her public face would be if they could witness this private moment.

My friend is not the first whose intentions have been misjudged by those who knew only part of the truth, rather than the whole truth. Take, for example, Bathsheba, once the wife of Uriah the Hittite; then his widow; then a wife of King David and mother of King Solomon. Many Bible commentators have judged Bathsheba guilty of causing King David's most devastating sin.

One spring night Bathsheba was outside her home bathing (that's *not* how she got her name) when King David caught a glimpse of her, sent for her, and committed adultery with her—causing a pregnancy that he was unable to cover up by any scheming. After David had her husband, Uriah, murdered on the battlefield, he made Bathsheba his wife.

Aside from being beautiful and taking a bath that evening, Bathsheba was not the main actor. Note that David did the sending and the scheming.

Bathsheba's name means *daughter of an oath.* One wonders what oath precipitated her birth. Was some promise fulfilled by her birth? Or was she born destined for some great task? Certainly that task was fulfilled as she eventually became Israel's queen mother. We don't know much about her background, just her father's name and that of her husband. If you carefully read the text in 2 Samuel

11 and 12, you'll see the Bible doesn't mention Bathsheba's state of mind during the adultery.

Imagine getting a visit from the king's messengers in the middle of the night. "Come with us; the king wishes to see you," they say. Could she refuse a king's request and say, "No, thank you, I'd rather not come"? What would this man after God's own heart (1 Samuel 13:14) want with her?

When she arrived at the palace and he wanted to sleep with her, could she have fled? Maybe. Maybe not. Guards would have been stationed outside the king's chambers. Did she give herself willingly?

Only God Himself knows. Yet through the ages, people have judged her guilty. Were she guilty, she could have sought God's forgiveness by her repentance. She may have done just that. It was David, though, whom the Scriptures record as repenting when the prophet Nathan brought the truth to light. When the infant conceived during the adultery died, it was the king who was quickly ready to move on; it was Bathsheba who grieved.

God did allow Bathsheba to be comforted, both by David and by the birth of Solomon. God redeemed this circumstance by using her as a wise counselor who helped preserve the promised throne for her son (1 Kings 1). Bathsheba even appears in the lineage of Christ—noted not by name, but as the mother of Solomon who "had been Uriah's wife" (Matthew 1:6).

Jesus cautioned, "Do not judge, and you will not be judged. Do not condemn, and you will not be condemned. Forgive, and you will be forgiven" (Luke 6:37). These are difficult words to put into practice when we think someone else's motives are perfectly clear—and perfectly wrong. Too often, it is we who are perfectly wrong. It's interesting, the juxtaposition of phrases in Jesus' statements. In order to be forgiven, we must forgive. In order to avoid judgment, we must avoid the temptation to judge others.

"How can I forgive someone who has used me? Why should I? He didn't ask for forgiveness." We don't want to accept the biblical principle that the apostle Paul puts succinctly, "You, therefore, have no excuse, you who pass judgment on someone else, for at whatever point you judge the other, you are condemning yourself, because you who pass judgment do the same things" (Romans 2:1).

Dear Father, You are the only One who knows the motive of every heart. I acknowledge what You already know: I have sinned against my sisters and brothers by condemning them in my heart, by judging them. I ask Your forgiveness; please do not judge me with the measure I have used to judge others. Amen.

28

DELILAH:
FEEBLE

Then Delilah said to Samson, "You have
made a fool of me; you lied to me. Come now,
tell me how you can be tied." *(Judges 16:10)*

The first day I walked into the building, I looked
like a miniature tourist. I peered up at the high
ceilings. Involuntarily my body shuddered at the
clash of thin metal doors slamming. At the insistence of a brash clanging sound, I scrambled down
the hall, heart pounding, eyes darting from wall to
wall at strangers—clusters of them—laughing and
slapping each other on the back.

So, this would be my new school. It was all so
intimidating; the setting and the other children
seemed larger than life. I seemed so small, so pow-
erless in my own eyes. Feigning my toughest
bravado, I steeled myself and acted as big as I
could. If I shared my school supplies with the other
kids, or if I helped them with their homework,
maybe then they would like me. But no, I was the
outsider; the only use they had for me was as a
punching bag during recess.

A few years ago, I walked back into that hall-
way, chuckling at the memory of my first weeks
there. True, I had been much shorter at the time, an
average-sized six year old. But it all looked so—
small. The locker doors only reached my shoulder

now. Their slamming sounded no more threatening than tin cans crushed underfoot. It suddenly didn't seem so important to have tried to impress a gaggle of grade-schoolers all those years ago.

My, how my perspective had changed. Those kids, those intimidating halls had been mere paper tigers. I had been able to blow past them with minor effort. They only had as much power over me as my own intimidation granted them.

Similarly, one of Israel's judges—Samson—was faced by a paper tiger. Instead of pushing her out of his path, though, he allowed her to become the conduit of his great downfall. Samson, you see, loved (or perhaps merely lusted after) Delilah.

Her name means "feeble." That should have been his first clue. His strong physical attraction toward her paralyzed his good judgment, and he sold himself into her evil "care" for the price of a few nights of pleasure. Odd that such a strong man, arguably one of the physically strongest men who ever lived, could be so critically weak in this one area.

The story is not at all flattering to Samson. The angel of the Lord visited his parents and announced that they, who had been childless, would have a son whose strength would come from God. The Lord was with him and blessed him. He fought and won many battles for God's people, Israel. But his private life was less than exemplary.

He fell in love with Delilah, who was either a Philistine (sworn enemies of Israel) or a Philistine sympathizer. Either way, for the bribe of a quantity of silver, she agreed to gain the secret of Samson's strength and betray him to the Philistine leaders.

So she began to wear him down, manipulating him by questioning his love for her. "How can you say, 'I love you,' when you won't confide in me?" she insisted (Judges 16:15). Instead of realizing that she couldn't have his best interests at heart, Samson played along, giving her false answers several times.

Finally, in desperation, worn down from all her nagging, "he told her everything. 'No razor has ever been used on my head,' he said, 'because I have been a Nazirite set apart to God since birth. If my head were shaved, my strength would leave me, and I would become as weak as any other man'" (Judges 16:17).

Commentators point out that the promise of Samson's birth and the directive that he be a life-long Nazirite never claim that his hair was the source of his strength. Samson's source of strength was God Himself. The Scripture says that when the Philistines cut Samson's hair and he lost his strength, it was because "the Lord had left him" (Judges 16:20). His connection *with* God equipped him to accomplish superhuman feats *for* God—who was to receive the glory.

So Samson allowed feeble arguments of a feeble woman to sever his relationship with God and thus to neutralize his strength. Had he the desire or the inner strength, Samson could have resisted Delilah's wiles; she would have toppled feebly had he confronted her.

This story is convicting to me. How many times do I give a circumstance or person more power than it actually has—because I fear it or (as in Samson's case) because I don't want to lose it? With all his mighty strength, Samson didn't recognize danger until it was too late. How often do I fail to recognize the workings of evil behind that which I love? How often do I give away all my secrets, compromise everything I hold dear, in a vain attempt to buy love or friendship? Nothing good could come of this kind of liaison.

As soon as Delilah had all the information and used it against Samson, she disappeared from the picture. The Bible does not mention her again. Samson—now blind, but whose hair began to grow back—has one last scene where he killed thousands of Philistines (and himself) by toppling their stadium. Perhaps he had learned a lesson—albeit a costly one. It is only through God's provision that we will find our strength. As the apostle Paul put it centuries later, "I can do everything God asks me to with the help of Christ who gives me the strength and power" (Philippians 4:13 TLB).

Perhaps I can learn this lesson from Samson's grave mistake, thereby saving myself from the humiliation of defeat by a paper tiger.

All-wise Father, help me recognize that only through Your strength can I do all things. Keep me from giving anything in this life the power to disconnect me from Your wisdom, strength, and love. Amen.

29

JEZEBEL:
BAAL IS HUSBAND

> There was never a man like Ahab, who sold
> himself to do evil in the eyes of the Lord, urged
> on by Jezebel his wife. (1 Kings 21:25)

Peer pressure. The phrase calls to mind preteen
or teenage years when many are tempted to depend too much upon others to define their worth
and value. We grown-ups caution teens not to give
in to pressures of drugs or cheating or sex. And we
feel self-righteous in doing such a service to our
"weaker" friends and relatives.

Do we really outgrow peer pressure when we
reach adulthood?

Some conformity is necessary for civilization.
And peers can pressure us into doing good things.
For example, I have peers who read the Bible with
more understanding than I, who have more effective prayer lives, who work more tirelessly. They
challenge me to reach toward excellence. This is
positive peer pressure.

But it's not all good.

Trying to catch her neighbors' eyes, she looked
to the right and to the left as the offering plate
passed by. With great ceremony she placed her offering envelope on the very top of the pile—face up
so the number of zeros after the one would attract
the attention of others in her pew. He sat beside

her, trying to avoid her eye. Yet he couldn't avoid a glance at her envelope. *I'm not letting her outdo me,* he thought. So he dug into his pocket and pulled out a large wad of bills that he was sure totaled more than her measly check. He placed them all in the plate and grinned widely. *That's one for me.*

Not your style? Well, what about our neighborhood competitions for the best lawn, the most manicured flower garden, the most expensive car, the largest home? Or our church potluck suppers where we shame each other into competing for the stomachs and palates of our fellow worshipers— only to race to the antacid bottle an hour later?

From kings and queens to peasants and surfs— not one of us has outgrown peer pressure. The frantic race to meet the expectations of others has just become more subtle, buried deeper into our psyches.

Picture every Walt Disney villainess who ever mixed her evil potions and cast her spells on her fellow fictional characters; roll all of these depraved women into one big ball, and you come close to the unthinkable cruelty of Jezebel. True to her name, *Baal is husband,* Jezebel chose to marry herself to evil. The Baals were heathen gods who were thought to demand from their subjects ritual human sacrifice, self-mutilation, and other abominable practices. Not only did Jezebel make the choice to serve the Baals for herself, but she influenced the eternal destruction of countless others as she compelled an entire country to conform to her pagan religion.

The daughter of a Sidonian king, the foreign princess Jezebel forged a marriage alliance with Israel's King Ahab. But Ahab did enough evil all by himself. He "considered it trivial to commit the sins" of previous Israelite kings (1 Kings 16:31). But his choice of Jezebel as queen caused him to sink to depths of unparalleled evil. He earned for himself the distinction: "There was never a man like Ahab, who sold himself to do evil in the eyes of the Lord, *urged on by Jezebel his wife*" (1 Kings 21:25, italics added).

In her court Jezebel maintained at least 850 false prophets, 400 of whom ate at her table. She massacred as many prophets of the true God as she could find. She hunted them down mercilessly. She threatened them. She intimidated them. Those who were left alive lived like hounded beasts—cowering in caves. Even the fearless prophet Elijah ran from Jezebel's sworn threat to exact revenge upon him.

If you have your Bible nearby, reread 1 Kings 18:16–40, which gives the account of Elijah's mighty stand against the prophets of Baal at Mount Carmel. Jezebel's false prophets provided a marvelous foil for a public display of Jehovah's power. Her prophets couldn't even call down fire to consume a dry sacrifice; Elijah's God, Jehovah, sent fire from heaven to consume his sacrifice that had been drenched in twelve huge jars of water. In fact, Jehovah's fire licked up water and soil, wood and stones. An all-consuming fire. As the onlookers witnessed the true powerlessness of the Baals in comparison with the unimaginable power of the living God, they bowed in worship to Jehovah. Then Elijah directed them in slaughtering Jezebel's prophets.

When Jezebel received word of this slaughter, she swore by her gods that she would kill Elijah.

But God would not allow Jezebel to destroy his servant Elijah. Instead, God saw to it that Jezebel's end was untimely and appropriately gory for such an amoral woman. A few years later, Jezebel's own servants threw her from the palace window, and her body was trampled on by horses and eaten by dogs (2 Kings 9:30–37). Only a few miscellaneous bones were left to be buried. Jezebel's reign of terror over Israel ended as Jehovah had foretold. God does exact His vengeance, His justice in the face of injustice —but He does so in His time and in His way.

Unlike my friends who offer strong, godly examples to emulate, the woman Jezebel chose to wield her considerable influence for evil. The legacy she left is that, down through the ages, her name has become synonymous with a malicious, vengeful woman. I wonder if that's what she had in mind?

God, I want to serve You only. And I want to use any influence I have upon others to cause them to serve You, as well. Help me to this end. Amen.

30

GOMER:
COMPLETE

When the Lord began to speak through
Hosea, the Lord said to him, "Go, take to yourself an adulterous wife and children of unfaithfulness, because the land is guilty of the vilest
adultery in departing from the Lord." (*Hosea 1:2*)

Autumn blows through the waning hours of
summer on the wings of the wind. Its companions are cooler temperatures, harvest leaves, and
football. In households across the land, TV sets
blare: "It's first and goal from the eight-yard line.
The quarterback barks the count; wide receivers
split right. . . . He takes a two-step drop . . . he
throws . . . it's complete for a touchdown." Fans
across the country celebrate as though they had
caught the winning pass.

Quarterbacks are rated on their pass-comple-
tion percentages. But they can't complete any pass
alone. Team members must block rushers and fake
handoffs, while the receivers run the called patterns
in order to be in the right place to receive the pass.
The receivers must have their hands and eyes coordinated to make a reception in the face of opposing
defenders.

What if a quarterback called this play in the
huddle? "OK, guys. Here's how it's gonna work. You
stay on the sidelines, and I'll take the ball, toss it
and dash down field to receive it all myself for the
score. Don't need any help, fellas. Thanks anyway!"

That guy would be off the field and under the eye of a CAT scan machine in ten seconds max.

As ridiculous as that scenario seems, some of us like to pretend we are self-sufficient, complete in ourselves, in need of no one else to make us whole. In this we are as deluded as our fictitious quarterback.

One woman in the Bible, Gomer—whose name means *complete*—thought she could take care of herself, thank-you-very-much. Proven wrong, she saw God use her sin as a nationally "broadcast" symbol of His people's unfaithfulness. Nevertheless, God used the love of her husband, Hosea, as a symbol of *His* unfailing faithfulness *to* His people.

In the waning days of Israel's Northern Kingdom, when the people were turning away from God and toward the abhorrent worship of idols, God instructed His prophet Hosea: "Go, take to yourself an adulterous wife and children of unfaithfulness, because the land is guilty of the vilest adultery in departing from the Lord" (Hosea 1:2).

Some modern-day commentators argue this was a symbolic marriage that took place in Hosea's imagination or that it was an allegory—that God would never ask His servant to do something so vile as to marry a prostitute. But biblical purists rightly respond,

> *All of these approaches to the passage issue from our offended sense of right and wrong. The plain meaning of the text is that Hosea married a prostitute at God's direct command. In this way, through his own tormented life Hosea could present a striking picture of the pain in God's heart because of the harlotries of His Covenant People.*[1]

In humble obedience, Hosea did as God commanded. He chose the prostitute Gomer and married her. She bore two sons and a daughter before she left Hosea to return to her seamy life of selling her body to the highest bidder.

We never hear Gomer's reasons for leaving Hosea. Perhaps she felt unclean and unworthy of Hosea's pure love. Perhaps her new life was so alien to her past that she could not adjust. Perhaps whining babies and day-to-day life seemed tedious in comparison to the thrills of her past life. Whatever her reasons, sin had a tight hold on her life, and she found herself living in squalor again—a slave of her adulterous "lover." Gomer paid a dear price for her sin. She gave up her comfortable home, her loving husband, any shred of self-respect, and even her personal freedom. But then God stepped in.

Hosea recorded God's new instructions: "The Lord said to me, 'Go, show your love to your wife again, though she is loved by another and is an adulteress. Love her as the Lord loves the Israelites, though they turn to other gods'" (3:1).

So Hosea went in search of his wife, found her in her filth, and bought her back for a slave's price. We aren't told how she responded to him, but we do know Hosea loved Gomer despite her unfaithfulness. Gomer's sinful choices provided a foil against which her husband's brilliant character qualities shone, illustrating God's love. Hosea offered unselfish love and forgiveness, but he held her to a high standard, telling her, "You are to live with me many days; you must not be a prostitute or be intimate with any man, and I will live with you" (3:3).

It's painfully easy to see ourselves in Gomer. How

often do we give up all the blessings that God offers to saunter down sin's sidewalks? How quickly do we find ourselves traversing unfriendly streets, falling down sin's open manholes, wishing for the safety of God's protection while sinking into the mucky gutter?

The good news is that God is faithful, though we are not. It is He who comes "to seek and to save that which was lost" (Luke 19:10 NASB), just as His servant Hosea went seeking his wayward wife.

Jesus said, "I am the vine; you are the branches. If a man remains in me and I in him, he will bear much fruit; apart from me you can do nothing" (John 15:5). So we who have bought into the world's notion that we can be complete on our own should take heed. Only in our dependence upon our faithful God can we be whole and complete, lacking nothing (Colossians 2:10).

Jesus offers us—His often unfaithful children—the same opportunity Hosea offered his repurchased wife: "As the Father has loved me, so have I loved you. Now remain in my love. If you obey my commands, you will remain in my love, just as I have obeyed my Father's commands and remain in his love. I have told you this so that my joy may be in you and that your joy may be complete" (John 15:9–11).

Jesus, strengthen me to remain in Your love, to remain faithful to You in this world that does everything it can to lure me away from You. Amen.

NOTE

1. "Book of Hosea," *Nelson's Illustrated Bible Dictionary* (Nashville: Thomas Nelson, 1986).

31

NOADIAH:
MEETING WITH JEHOVAH

> Remember Tobiah and Sanballat, O my God,
> because of what they have done; remember
> also the prophetess Noadiah and the rest of the
> prophets who have been trying to intimidate
> me. (Nehemiah 6:14)

How do you want to be remembered?
With that question, I begin a speech about recording your memories and passing them along to generations to follow. It's a presentation I've given numerous times, because adults who are in or past middle age are starting to think about how they can make a lasting impact on this world.

We all relate to stories about people like us. Jesus put this truth into practice through the parables He told to the multitudes. He paired incomprehensible truths about heaven with easily understood earthly settings so that even the uneducated masses could come to a deeper understanding of the character of God the Father.

Each of us has a story. A history. A tale to tell about our walk through life. And each of us has a driving passion to leave something of ourselves for posterity—something for which we will be remembered. No one will experience life just as you will, or as I will. It's a marvel that testifies to the awesome love of our Creator. He designed each of us uniquely, and He designed each of our lives on an individual course.

Those of us who are followers of Jesus Christ have an added incentive to tell our stories. Not only do we want to be remembered when we have left this earth, but more important, we want to see our loved ones follow us as we follow Christ. We want others to see God's history of faithfulness to us, so they may be encouraged to trust Him with their lives. This being so, we need to make the daily choice to lift up Christ, do nothing out of selfish ambition, and offer to Him any glory we would otherwise be tempted to seize as our own.

Tragically, some individuals choose to be remembered for things that do anything but bring God glory. Such is the case with a false prophetess in the Old Testament. Her name was Noadiah: *meeting with Jehovah.* She was named with the hope of a glorious future; instead, she chose to leave a legacy of eternal doom.

She lived during one of the most exhilarating times in Israel's history. It was after the seventy years of captivity, after the nation had been invited to return home, after their forced servitude to the Babylonian empire. Persia had overthrown Babylon. With the Persian king's blessing, Nehemiah had returned to the rubble of Jerusalem to rebuild the city walls. He and his contemporaries, including Ezra the priest, assembled a work crew to accomplish their goal. Earlier, Zerubbabel (grandson of the last king of Judah) had led a multiyear effort to rebuild God's temple in Jerusalem.

God had made it clear in prophecies before the captivity that it was His will that the people return to their land after seventy years of exile. In fact, when Zerubbabel led the first band of captives home, the prophet Haggai chastised him for spending too much time building his own home before rebuilding God's earthly dwelling place (Haggai 1:2–4). Clearly, the work of the rebuilders was consistent with God's stated will for His people.

For God's newly returned exiles, it should have been "the best of times." And yet, because of the influence of prophets who allied themselves with the opposition forces, it became "the worst of times."

Throughout history, Satan has used every means at his disposal to try to thwart God's purpose. Noadiah is named as one who opposed Nehemiah's work. Rather than *meeting with Jehovah,* the prophetess Noadiah was *meeting with the enemy.*

Noadiah's intimidation, her collaboration with enemy agents who threatened Nehemiah's life, and her association with their guerrilla tactics forced the builders to divide their forces—some worked on the wall while others wielded swords. In fact, all the workers had swords close at hand.

Knowing he was acting at God's direction, Nehemiah responded to the threats by crying out to God in prayer. Seven times in the book that bears his name, Nehemiah prays that God will "remember" him and not fail to act on his behalf. He also prays that God will remember Noadiah for her evil actions. Other false prophets were lumped into one group; but Noadiah was named specifically. She must have been an especially vocal antagonist.

God would not then, nor will He ever, allow His purpose to be thwarted. He granted Nehemiah wisdom, strength, and courage to overcome the opposition's schemes. The wall was rebuilt in just two months—a fantastic feat and tribute to God's faithfulness to be remembered for countless generations.

Even today, our Lord offers these same provisions to His people. Remember the apostle John's words, "You are from God, little children, and have overcome them; because greater is He who is in you than he who is in the world" (1 John 4:4 NASB). God will remember His faithful followers; He will not allow them to be intimidated.

But what of those who place themselves in concert with enemy forces? God will indeed remember them—not for good, but instead for their evil.

So we end this look at Noadiah's legacy back where we began. How do we want to be remembered? When we stand before God, will we be remembered for good or for evil? Will He welcome us into His eternal joy because we have fought faithfully, side by side with His warriors; or will our disloyalty to His forces send us to eternal doom? Or will we suffer disappointment in realizing a third option: making it into heaven but seeing our works burned up as they are shown to be irrelevant or hurtful to the kingdom (1 Corinthians 3:12–15)? It's my choice, and it's yours.

Almighty God, I choose to align myself with Your forces. I want to be remembered on earth and in heaven as Your faithful follower. Make me worthy of that high calling. Amen.

32

HERODIAS:
HEROIC

For John had been saying to Herod, "It is
not lawful for you to have your brother's wife."
So Herodias nursed a grudge against John and
wanted to kill him. (*Mark 6:18–19*)

In our single adult Sunday school class we spent
several months studying prayer. The section that
engendered the most heated exchanges within the
group was the study of hindrances to prayer.

The Scripture was Mark 11:25: "And when you
stand praying, if you hold anything against anyone,
forgive him, so that your Father in heaven may forgive you your sins."

"Do you mean you can't be forgiven if you fail
to forgive?" one classmate asked.

"Well, Jesus said 'so that' you'll be forgiven," I
replied. Then I read aloud what the curriculum
writer said: "While, through acceptance of Christ,
one stands delivered from the *penalty* of his sins
(Hebrews 8:12), can God deal with His child on the
basis of forgiveness while that child harbors ill will
in his heart toward others?"[1] The obvious answer,
we agreed, is "no."

"But what if they haven't asked for forgiveness
and don't deserve it? It sounds like you're letting
them off easy—they're not paying for their wrongs.
I don't see how holding a grudge can be bad if

someone has sinned against you," insisted another classmate.

How would you answer?

Let's look at the degeneration of a heart that harbored a grudge against another person. Let's look at Herodias, Herod's brother's wife.

Her name means *heroic*. She was more like our culture's definition of heroic than like God's definition. She had money. She had power. She had position. She had little accountability for her actions—and she wanted even less. She was living in an ungodly union with her husband's brother, a situation that, as John the Baptist kept pointing out, was clearly sinful.

I can imagine Herodias's thoughts: *For some maddening reason, Herod likes to keep this John the Baptist around. What if he begins acting on John's teachings? Where would that land me? Maybe I'll be thrown back to my mealy-mouthed husband, Philip. Why would I want to go back to him when the true power lies with Herod?*

She brooded. She simmered. She schemed. She allowed the hatred to grow. Although she was the one in need of cleansing and forgiveness, and although John had merely pointed out an obvious sin in her life, Herodias nurtured the grudge she held against him. She bided her time until she could rid the world of this pious, holy man. His existence sickened her. Probably it made her feel a tinge of guilt, too, if her seared conscience was yet capable of any feeling.

Then the opportunity presented itself: Herod was throwing a gala. And Herodias sent in her daughter Salome to dance for the king's guests. This pleased the king so much that he promised the girl anything she asked. Herodias swooped in and influenced the girl to ask for the head of John the Baptist on a platter. The promise made before his guests, Herod believed he had to comply to save face.

And such was the end of the forerunner of Christ, John the Baptist.

In our Sunday school class, in answer to the question about nurturing grudges, we looked at Jesus' parable of the servant who was forgiven a debt he could never pay, but then refused to forgive his debtor a small pittance. These are Jesus' words about the end of that servant:

> Then the master called the servant in. "You wicked servant," he said, "I canceled all that debt of yours because you begged me to. Shouldn't you have had mercy on your fellow servant just as I had on you?" In anger his master turned him over to the jailers to be tortured, until he should pay back all he owed. This is how my heavenly Father will treat each of you unless you forgive your brother from your heart. (Matthew 18:32–35)

Herodias and her grudge did succeed in destroying the earthly life of the hated John. Yet John will be in heaven for all ages. And Herodias? Unless she eventually heeded John's call for repentance, she will burn in hell for all eternity. Was the bitter grudge worth her own eternal destruction? How much better it would have been for Herodias to have sought God's forgiveness when confronted, and then, like David with the prophet Nathan, appreciated God's messenger for being honest enough to risk the confrontation.

The one who nurtures a grudge—who refuses to forgive from her heart and to seek forgiveness—grants bitterness fertile soil in which to grow. Soon, this bearer becomes a slave to bitterness, resentment, and anger. If not pulled up by its roots, the grudge will consume its holder (like the man-eating plant in the play *Little Shop of Horrors*), and the eventual cost will be the holder's own soul.

Lord, it is too easy, too human, to allow grudges and unforgiveness to have a place in my heart. I see now how these can choke out my relationship with You, so I ask that You equip and enable me to pull them up by their roots and to forgive them all. Amen.

NOTE

1. Keith L. Brooks, *How to Pray* (Chicago: Moody, 1961), 25.

33

SAPPHIRA:
SAPPHIRE

> Now a man named Ananias, together with his wife Sapphira, also sold a piece of property. With his wife's full knowledge he kept back part of the money for himself, but brought the rest and put it at the apostles' feet. *(Acts 5:1–2)*

The Creator must love things of great beauty. His palette was alive with colors and shapes and textures and aromas that only He could have conceived.

Consider the purples of a rainbow or the "circus of autumn." Consider the unmistakable aromas of bread baking or of a campfire crackling happily. Consider the contrasts of the ground: the red clay of Kentucky and the dusty earth tones of the Sahara, the warm green ground cover of the tropics and the sharp white ice of the Arctic regions.

Among my favorite beauties of God's creation are those stones we call gems. They sparkle and reflect prisms of light. They come in colors as varied as a rainbow. Fiery diamonds, colorless until they reflect the light. Rich red rubies and garnets. Sea green emeralds. Amber topaz stones. Deep blue sapphires.

I especially love sapphires, because my father bought me a sapphire ring for my twenty-fifth birthday. When I admire this ring, I think of the many times sapphires are mentioned in Scriptures. (They must be one of God's favorites too.) When

Moses and the seventy elders of Israel saw the Lord in Exodus 24:10 they saw that: "Under his feet was something like a pavement made of sapphire, clear as the sky itself." When it came time to design the high priest's garments, a sapphire stone was included in the second of four rows of precious jewels to bedeck the breastpiece (Exodus 28:18). Then, when Ezekiel had his vision of the "wheel within a wheel," he saw God on a throne that appeared to be made of sapphire (Ezekiel 1:26). Finally, in John's vision of the city of God recorded in Revelation, one of the layers of the wall was made of sapphire (21:19).

Certainly, God values the gemstones He created, sapphires among them. And He valued another sapphire He created, Sapphira *(sapphire)*. Unfortunately, she did not live up to the pure and shining splendor befitting her name.

Sapphira and her husband, Ananias, lived in the first century, after Jesus was resurrected and ascended into heaven. Their story is recorded in the book of the Acts of the Apostles. The context is that all the believers in Christ were sharing their possessions with each other. "There were no needy persons among them. For from time to time those who owned lands or houses sold them, brought the money from the sales and put it at the apostles' feet, and it was distributed to anyone as he had need" (Acts 4:34–35).

No one forced the believers to sell their property and share the proceeds; they did so out of love for their Master. It was a glorious time of unity in the body of Christ. His followers were caring for each other as for themselves. Yet the weeds of selfishness had not been entirely uprooted.

Wanting the glory of being known as generous,

Ananias and Sapphira sold their property. Bringing some of the proceeds to the apostles and saving the remainder for himself, Ananias (with Sapphira's full knowledge) claimed he was bringing the entire sum.

God allowed Peter to discern the falsehood in Ananias:

> Then Peter said, "Ananias, how is it that Satan has so filled your heart that you have lied to the Holy Spirit and have kept for yourself some of the money you received for the land? Didn't it belong to you before it was sold? And after it was sold, wasn't the money at your disposal? What made you think of doing such a thing? You have not lied to men but to God." (Acts 5:3–4)

What was the consequence of lying to God—especially in such a public way? Immediately, Ananias "fell down and died" (Acts 5:5).

No sooner had some men buried her husband than Sapphira appeared before the apostles—the three-hour delay likely choreographed by the couple to allow Sapphira to receive accolades in line with her "great" generosity.

Word had not reached Sapphira regarding her husband's fate. So Peter tested her, asking whether the amount Ananias brought to the apostles was the full purchase price. Sapphira held to the lie her husband had told. "Peter said to her, 'How could you agree to test the Spirit of the Lord? Look! The feet of the men who buried your husband are at the door, and they will carry you out also.' At that moment she fell down at his feet and died" (Acts 5:9–10).

Ananias and Sapphira had not taken to heart Jesus' warning, "Do not store up for yourselves treasures on earth, where moth and rust destroy, and where thieves break in and steal. But store up for yourselves treasures in heaven, where moth and rust do not destroy, and where thieves do not break in and steal. For where your treasure is, there your heart will be also" (Matthew 6:19–21). This couple's heart was set on the wrong treasure. They were pursuing earthly rewards—puffing themselves up for human accolades.

Jesus calls His followers to value His kingdom above anything in this earthly realm. He told this parable to emphasize His point: "Again, the kingdom of heaven is like a merchant seeking beautiful pearls, who, when he had found one pearl of great price, went and sold all that he had and bought it" (Matthew 13:45–46 NKJV).

But the cause of Sapphira's death was not just her failure to value God's kingdom over earthly treasure. She died because she lied to God. She had forgotten Jesus' declaration, "What you have said in the dark will be heard in the daylight, and what you have whispered in the ear in the inner rooms will be proclaimed from the roofs" (Luke 12:3).

God knows. He is fully aware of everything whispered in secret. And one day (sometimes immediately, sometimes not) all that is said in secret will be revealed. Will that be a glad day or a sad day for you?

Jesus, purify my thoughts, my motives, my inner life, so that on the day when my secrets are unveiled I will be found worthy of the pearl of great price—Your jewel-bedecked kingdom. Amen.

34

MARY, MOTHER OF JESUS: BOND OF THE FAMILY

But Mary treasured up all these things and pondered them in her heart. (*Luke 2:19*)

My mother had emergency surgery early this year. When she was released from the hospital, her surgeon ordered her to take two weeks of complete rest. After two days of bed rest, she began to feel well enough to shuffle gingerly about the house.

For the remainder of her time on injured reserve, she sat at her desk, busy with what she told me was "paperwork." Doing my best to do a portion of the work she does every day to hold our family together, I didn't snoop on her mysterious activities.

On the tenth evening after her surgery, I returned home from work to find a package on my bed wrapped in two grocery bags. Curious, I didn't even put down my briefcase before opening the bag. Inside was a bulging scrapbook. Mom had been treasuring up mementos of my life's achievements. Feeling like a contestant on "This Is Your Life," I paged through the book's contents: report cards, programs from concerts and recitals, crayon drawings, graduation booklets, ticket stubs, swatches of favorite garments. She had spent her confinement creating a treasure book of my life.

That got me thinking: what would Mary's treasure book of her son Jesus' life look like? He called her "Mother." Like my mom, she was the *bond of the family,* at least of His earthly family. (Since this book has many women named Mary—*bitterness*—or a variation of that name, I am "defining" the next several Marys with a sense of who they are rather than the actual definition of the name.) Sometimes Jesus' mother acted with wisdom beyond her years, at other times she failed to understand His ministry, but always she "treasured up all these things and pondered them in her heart" (Luke 2:19).

A loving mother, chosen by God's inerrant design, Mary was integrally involved in her son's life. She had much to ponder—much to include in her son's treasure book. The appearance of the angel Gabriel must have frightened the teenaged Mary, yet she indicated her pliability: "I am the Lord's servant," she answered Gabriel. "May it be to me as you have said" (Luke 1:38). With those words, she agreed to participate in a plan that had begun to play out millennia before, at the creation of the world—a plan she could not fully comprehend. Mary's son was the fulfillment of the prophecy God gave to Eve after sin entered the world in Eden (Genesis 3:15), the fulfillment of prophecies given to God's servants down through the ages.

Mary treasured the memories of giving birth to Jesus in a smelly stable and of the ragtag band of filthy shepherds who appeared that night to gawk at her tiny son. She treasured the words of Simeon and Anna who prophesied in the temple court about how her son would cause the rise and fall of many within Israel, and how a sword would pierce her heart (Luke 2:34–35). It was beginning to sting already.

Her book about Jesus would include a notation about wealthy astrologers from the East, who came to pay homage to Jesus, and about the family's middle-of-the-night flight to Egypt to protect the child from Herod's fury. She would remember unspeakable grief with the mothers of Bethlehem whose babies Herod executed because of her son.

As Jesus grew, Mary would recall that the dailyness of life made Him seem more like *her* child than God's Son. So when, after three days of anxious searching, she and Joseph found twelve-year-old Jesus in the temple of Jerusalem asking questions of the teachers of the law (students didn't ask questions; only teachers did), she didn't understand her son's response: "'Why were you searching for me?' he asked. 'Didn't you know I had to be in my Father's house?'" (Luke 2:49). Again she found herself treasuring these things in her heart (Luke 2:51).

She was at the wedding in neighboring Cana when Jesus performed His first recorded public miracle. She begged Him to do something to save the host the embarrassment of running out of wine; it was she who instructed the servants of the household to do whatever Jesus told them to do. After He had turned water into wine and the wedding was over, Mary spent time with Jesus and His disciples (John 2:1–12). (I wonder whether she kept a wine-stained napkin as a reminder of this miracle.)

Then she began misunderstanding His ministry again. She and His brothers came to take Him into their custody because His conduct was frightening them. "They went to take charge of him, for they said, 'He is out of his mind'" (Mark 3:21).

Mary's loyalty and love for her son prevailed, though, as did His for her. At the Cross where Jesus was enduring the shame and untold agony of bearing the sins of the world, Mary knelt nearby weeping —all these scenes running through her mind. She could hear His tortured breaths. She could smell His lifeblood, hear it splattering on the ground. Even here, Jesus saw to her needs, entrusting His mother to His beloved disciple John. Painfully, gesturing with His head toward John, He gasped, "Dear woman, here is your son" and to John, "Here is your mother" (John 19:26–27).

Mary was born as one of the fallen human race that Jesus came to earth to redeem; it was for her salvation, too, that her son died. She had the same choice before her that each of us has—to trust Jesus to save us from the penalty of our sins, or to turn away from Him, setting ourselves up for eternal punishment.

At first all of this seemed a jumble to her mind. The pieces didn't fit together to make a complete picture. But as she was pondering it all, a glimmer of understanding illumined the scenes she had been treasuring in her heart. After Jesus' resurrection and ascension, we see Mary in the Upper Room with the men and women who had followed Jesus, joining in constant prayer and awaiting the infilling of the Holy Spirit (Acts 1:14). She had made the choice to move from doubt to faith. She had a new bond to a new family, the eternal family bound together in service to her beloved son—and her God.

Dear Jesus, thank You for choosing an earthly mother who would be an example to me of how to move from doubt to faith. Thank You for patiently loving me through my seasons of doubt and for restoring my faith. Amen.

35

MARTHA:
LADY OF THE HOUSE

As Jesus and his disciples were on their way,
he came to a village where a woman named
Martha opened her home to him. *(Luke 10:38)*

If you have ever visited the Smithsonian Museum
of American History in Washington, D.C., you
probably have been dazzled by the array of classic
china patterns that have served as the official fine
dinnerware in each first lady's White House. Each
pattern reflects a first lady's distinctive personality
and gives a glimpse into her method of entertaining
international dignitaries.

Similarly, when a new president moves into the
White House, his wife often redecorates the mansion. Who could forget Jackie Kennedy's nationally
televised tour of the White House after her magnificent redecoration was completed?

I own a copy of a gilded 1881 volume titled
The Ladies of the White House. In it author Laura C.
Holloway takes readers inside the homes of the
presidents from Washington to Garfield. Holloway
begins by saying: "The Ladies of the White House
have had no biographers . . . the world took little
cognizance of them beyond noting the entertain-
ment they gave, and the success that attended their
dinners and receptions."[1] Holloway also notes that
despite their relative anonymity, these women

"were powerful adjuncts to their [husbands'] popularity, and exerted great influence over their lives." By implication, then, they exerted great influence over the country.

First ladies of the United States are not the only ones who have been trivialized by society's categorizing them as useful only for entertaining guests. Most of us who have been in the church for many years have heard dozens of sermons about Martha, sister of Lazarus, who was too busy serving dinner to sit and listen at Christ's feet. Although we have rightly learned from these sermons that time with Jesus is more important than anything we could do *for* Him, many of us have also gained the misimpression that Martha's service was not of value to Christ and to her household.

Martha, while her name (similar to Mary's) translates as "she was rebellious," was the *lady of the house*. She was involved in several scenes of Jesus' earthly life, scenes where she demonstrated grace and the value to Jesus of her loving service.

We first meet Martha in Luke 10:38–42 as a woman who "opened her home" to Jesus. She allowed her home to become a place where the Master could sit and teach—a comfortable platform for His ministry. It was during this occasion that Jesus chastised Martha—not for her service, but for her attitude. Listen to some of the words Luke records: "But Martha was distracted by all the preparations that had to be made" (v. 40). Jesus put his finger on the heart of the matter, telling her, "You are worried and upset about many things" (v. 41). Her distraction, worry, and agitation were causing her to sin.

The Scriptures often remind Jesus' followers not to worry, to be "anxious for nothing," to focus our attention on Him. When we do that, all our other needs will be cared for. This was the lesson He taught Martha that day—not that her work lacked value, but that her spirit needed the peace that comes from knowing Him.

We meet Martha again after her brother Lazarus died. John records that "Jesus loved Martha and her sister and Lazarus" (John 11:5). It's interesting that John names Martha first. Also note "When Martha heard that Jesus was coming, she went out to meet him" (v. 20). She was looking for comfort and had deep questions on her heart—naturally, she ran to Jesus.

Apparently, Martha had been listening intently to the messages Jesus had been preaching, because during her conversation with Him after her brother's death, Martha made a remarkable statement of belief in Jesus. "I believe that you are the Christ, the Son of God, who was to come into the world" (John 11:27). When Peter made that same confession, Jesus told him, "Flesh and blood did not reveal this to you, but My Father who is in heaven" (Matthew 16:17 NASB). So Martha received the same revelation from God that Peter received.

Then Martha was present, with her sister Mary and numerous Jews, when Jesus raised Lazarus from the dead. Martha: the practical one. When Jesus asked for the stone to be rolled away from the tomb, she wrinkled her nose, arched her eyebrows, and blurted out, "Lord, by this time he stinketh" (John 11:39 KJV). (I know Martha didn't speak King James English, but it sounds appropriate here.)

Finally, in one of the last scenes before His crucifixion, a weary, heavyhearted Jesus came to Martha's home once more: for repose, respite, respect. Here was a place where He was safe, where He could enjoy a dinner in His honor with people whom He loved—and who loved Him in return. Again, Martha served. But this time, she appears not to have been frazzled. This time she was offering her gift of hospitality, one of the many gifts of the Spirit to believers, in service to her Lord. This time Martha did not expect her sister to express her love to the Lord through serving a meal. This freed Mary to make her own expression of love to Jesus—through anointing Him with costly perfume, unknowingly in preparation for His burial.

Martha was diligent and practical with a meticulous sense of hospitality. She coordinated many details efficiently and effectively. She was generous and full of faith in Christ. Most of all, when she received Jesus' rebuke, she made the appropriate changes in her heart, attitude, and actions. Our Lord will likely have cause to rebuke each of us. May we each handle those rebukes gracefully, in a manner befitting a lady of any house—from the suburbs to the White House.

Lord, may I serve my family and others who enter my household as if I am serving You. May they see my love for You through my service to them. Amen.

NOTE

1. Laura C. Holloway, *The Ladies of the White House* (Philadelphia: Bradley & Company, 1881), 3.

36

MARY, SISTER OF LAZARUS: SISTER

> Then Mary took about a pint of pure nard, an expensive perfume; she poured it on Jesus' feet and wiped his feet with her hair. And the house was filled with the fragrance of the perfume. (*John 12:3*)

I grew up in an old-fashioned church, largely composed of four families. Most of the families had intermarried; everyone was related to the others by blood, by marriage, or at least by family history. My grandfather had been a teenager living with one of the families when the whole household received and accepted the message of salvation—and he with them. This family was one of the "big four" in the church.

Because of this tight relation, it was easy for even a small child to think of the church as one big family. Some of the men and women my parents' age I called "aunt," or "uncle," even though technically we weren't related. As a term of respect, we younger people called the other older members by their first names with the term "Sister" or "Brother" in front of the name (Sister Helen, Brother Tony, etc.).

It wasn't until later years that I came to realize the depth of meaning conveyed in these simple terms. In a real sense, more real than anything else on this earth, these men and women of the church are my brothers and sisters. One day, we will kneel in worship before God's throne, side by side, with equal footing, each having entered this unearthly family by way of a new birth made possible by Jesus' sacrificial death.

In Matthew 12 Jesus' mother and brothers sent word that they wanted to talk to Him. The Master looked around and gestured to His loyal followers, "Whoever does the will of my Father in heaven is my brother and sister and mother" (v. 50). What an amazing concept. Jesus called the women who followed Him sisters: Joanna, Susanna, Mary Magdalene, Martha and her sister Mary, and many others whose names history doesn't record. These women were related to Christ, part of His spiritual family. Mary, who had been named for the very human *seed of rebellion,* Jesus now considered His *sister.*

Three scenes in the Gospels provide insight into this sister in Christ. First, when Martha opened their home to Jesus, Mary chose to sit and listen at Jesus' feet—to drink in the deep, soul-quenching truths He spoke—rather than to rush around the kitchen and make preparations for the feast with her sister. Jesus respected Mary's heart-impulsive choice, chiding the complaining Martha with the powerful statement: "Mary has chosen what is better, and it will not be taken away from her" (Luke 10:42). Mary was a thinker, a listener. She expressed her love for the Master by spending quality time with Him, paying rapt attention to His every word.

We see Mary again in the days following the death of her brother Lazarus. Finally, after Lazarus had been in the tomb four days, the family's friend Jesus arrived at the outskirts of the town of

Bethany, where they lived. Martha ran to Jesus, displaying remarkable faith in Him ("I know that even now God will give you whatever you ask"—John 11:22) and launching into a theological discussion about death and resurrection.

Mary waited until Jesus called for her. When she ran to Him, she didn't begin a theological discussion. Instead, she fell at His feet weeping. Her tears broke the heart of the Master. "When Jesus saw her weeping . . . he was deeply moved in spirit and troubled. . . . Jesus wept" (John 11:33, 35).

Note Jesus' differing responses to the two sisters in the same situation. To Martha He provided wisdom; to Mary He offered shared grief. To both He offered great comfort. He comes to each of us where we are; He understands our unique temperaments; He meets our needs as only One who fully understands ever could.

In this scene we catch a glimpse of Mary's tender heart, her sensitive nature. Note the significance of Jesus, the Son of God, weeping with Sister Mary. That the One with the power to call Lazarus back to life weeps with us should bring us great comfort. When emergencies occur in our lives, Jesus will not always resolve our dilemma, but He will always empathize with our heart cries and soothe our tears.

In John 12, we see Mary's family one more time: Lazarus was very much alive, sitting with Jesus; Martha was serving; and Mary had her own way of thanking the Master for all He had done for her: "Then Mary took about a pint of pure nard, an expensive perfume; she poured it on Jesus' feet and wiped his feet with her hair. And the house was filled with the fragrance of the perfume" (John 12:3).

Perhaps Mary's tender heart took notice of a slight change in Jesus. He was resolute now. His spirit was heavy with the burden He was about to take upon His shoulders. Perhaps she noted a hint in His visage of the grief Jesus would experience in the Garden of Gethsemane. Most people wouldn't notice the difference. But she knew Him too well. He had entrusted her with too many truths about His kingdom in the hours she had spent with Him. Feeling His pain, how could she do anything less than try to lighten her Master's burden?

Sensitive Mary, expressing the purity of her love for Jesus, took her most valuable possession and poured it out on Jesus' feet—the same feet before which she had sat to listen to His words. Sisterly love in its finest form. She lavished the best she had upon her Lord.

Jesus alone understood the significance of her action. When Judas Iscariot objected to this "waste," Jesus responded, "Leave her alone. . . . It was intended that she should save this perfume for the day of my burial" (v. 7). Mary had spent the time building a deep relationship with Jesus, so it was she who received the unparalleled privilege of serving Him by anointing His body for burial. Perhaps this action was foreshadowed in Jesus' earlier words: "Mary has chosen what is better, and it will not be taken away from her."

Lord, thank You for calling me Your sister. Thank You for the many truths You have entrusted to me. May I choose the better—today and always. Amen.

37

MARY MAGDALENE:
THE TOWER

> Then the disciples went back to their homes, but Mary stood outside the tomb crying. As she wept, she bent over to look into the tomb and saw two angels in white, seated where Jesus' body had been, one at the head and the other at the foot. *(John 20:10–12)*

It reaches 1,454 feet into the sky and occupies an acre of land. It houses a working population of 16,500 people who can view the outside world from any one of 16,000 tinted windows. It has a 103-cab elevator system (plus 24 freight elevators) and was constructed from (among other things) 76,000 tons of steel, 2 million cubic feet of concrete, 1,500 miles of electrical wiring, and 80 miles of elevator cable.

Completed in 1974 and known for years as the world's tallest building, it is the 110-story modern-day engineering marvel—Chicago's Sears Tower.

A skyscraper like the Sears Tower must be anchored deep into the bedrock; its foundation must be sure in any conditions to support its own hefty weight, let alone its structure entrusted with the weight and lives of more than 16,000 people. Housed in the Windy City, this structure also needed special rigid tubing around its perimeter to provide sufficient windbracing.

Without overspiritualizing, I can see a few parallels between this tower and the Christian life. First, we must have as our foundation a deeply anchored faith in Jesus Christ. Then, we need His supportive, loving arms around us to brace us from the tornado-force wind currents that threaten to topple anything that is not battened down.

These are lessons one faithful follower of Jesus learned during His earthly ministry. She experienced His saving grace and His delivering hand from the tornado winds of the dark spirit world that nearly destroyed her; she was a witness to His death and the first human entrusted to spread the message of His resurrection. She was Mary from the city of Magdala, the city whose name meant *the tower.*

Once she had been true to her given name: Mary, *rebellion.* Her body had been home to seven demons (Mark 16:9); one could only imagine the havoc these spirits wreaked on their hostess. But then Jesus came to her village: Magdala, a prosperous fishing region on the Sea of Galilee between Tiberias and Capernaum. He cast those demons out of her and freed her. Once delivered, Mary became true to her second name: *the tower.*

As one who had been delivered from much by the only One who could offer such complete freedom, Mary Magdalene loved her Lord with a deep, abiding love. She traveled with Jesus as one of His faithful entourage, following Him from town to village, hearing Him proclaim the Good News, helping support His ministry out of her own means (Luke 8:1–3).

When the rulers seized Jesus and crucified Him, there was Mary, standing with the other women who "had followed Jesus from Galilee to care for his needs" (Matthew 27:55). When Joseph of Arimathea took Jesus' bloody, bruised, beaten body and placed it in his own tomb, Mary Magdalene and another Mary stayed close, watching, waiting for their turn to minister to Jesus' body. But it was too late that evening; the Sabbath laws forbade work such as this from sundown Friday to sundown Saturday.

Sunday morning—at dawn—Mary Magdalene was among the small procession of women who set out for the tomb with newly purchased spices to anoint Jesus' body. She knew Pilate had placed soldiers at the Lord's tomb to keep His followers from stealing the body; she knew a huge stone had been rolled over the entrance; she knew she was putting her life in danger even being associated with the crucified Jesus. Yet she came. As early as she could get there, she came to the tomb.

Perhaps as a reward for her tenacity, God bestowed on this woman a great honor: Mary Magdalene was the first to see the resurrected Christ. She touched Him. Spoke with Him. Was commissioned by Him to carry the world's most wonderful message.

Mark records the scene rather matter-of-factly: "When Jesus rose early on the first day of the week, he appeared first to Mary Magdalene" (Mark 16:9).

From John's more detailed account, we know that Mary stood outside the tomb crying. Suddenly two angels appeared and asked why she was crying. Then Jesus appeared to her, but through her tears she mistook Him for a gardener—until something in the way He called her name called her to attention:

> Jesus said to her, "Mary." She turned toward him and cried out in Aramaic, "Rabboni!" (which means Teacher).
>
> Jesus said, "Do not hold on to me, for I have not yet returned to the Father. Go instead to my brothers and tell them, 'I am returning to my Father and your Father, to my God and your God.'"
>
> Mary Magdalene went to the disciples with the news: "I have seen the Lord!" And she told them that he had said these things to her. (John 20:16–18)

The last to leave the cross, the first to return to the tomb was the one Jesus sent to announce His resurrection to the disciples.

Look at the change Jesus Christ made in Mary Magdalene's life: She had felt her own insufficiency apart from Christ, but He had transformed her into a strong tower, infused her with His love, equipped her with a courage that resulted in unwavering loyalty.

If He could do that for her . . .

Loving Lord Jesus, thank You for honoring the loyalty of the woman Mary Magdalene, who served You with her whole heart. May I serve You likewise. Amen.

38

JOANNA:
GOD IS A GRACIOUS GIVER

> The Twelve were with him, and also some
> women who had been cured of evil spirits and
> diseases: Mary (called Magdalene) from whom
> seven demons had come out; Joanna the wife
> of Cuza, the manager of Herod's household;
> Susanna; and many others. These women were
> helping to support them out of their own
> means. (*Luke 8:1–3*)

When I consider the concept of God's gracious
provision for His people, I can think of no
better showcase than the story of baby Nathan
Wallestad.

Nina and Craig wanted to have a baby together.
But that wasn't in God's plan. Instead, their desire
set them on a journey into the world of international
adoption. As they were completing the approval
process at one agency, they hit an immovable road-
block: Craig's mild epilepsy disqualified the couple
from adopting with this agency.

Devastated, Nina began e-mailing her friends,
asking us to pray for God's guidance. Her friends e-
mailed their friends across the country, and soon a
national prayer chain was operating. God then led
the couple to an agency where the epilepsy was not
an issue. Within weeks, Nina and Craig received a
history of a not-quite-six-month-old Russian boy.
Here's how Nina described him: "The still photos
show a little sandy-haired, dark-eyed baby looking
curiously at the camera. His smile is big yet shy,

and lights up his face. Whenever he smiles, his whole body smiles." Obviously, the couple fell in love with this baby at first sight. They agreed to adopt him.

Their travel to Russia for a court date was set, and Nina told everyone about their new son, whom they named Nathan (*given*). But days before they were to leave, Russian courts strictly limited American adoptions, beginning with those scheduled the week of Nathan's. Again, Nina enlisted prayer support. A court date opened up miraculously.

Now they worried: Would they find Nathan (then eight months old) healthy? Would he accept them as his parents? Again, God was providing answers. Nathan passed his U.S. entrance exam without needing even one shot (an unheard-of blessing). And Nina wrote from Russia, "The best miracle of all is how quickly Nathan seems to have bonded with both Mama and Papa (although right now Mama is the parent of choice by a small margin!)."

God filled the empty arms of these parents with a child who needed their love; God filled the heart of this abandoned infant with the overflowing love of godly parents.

The Wallestads are only among the latest in a long line of Christ's followers to see His gracious provision firsthand. One New Testament disciple, Joanna, was named in acknowledgment of this truth: *Jehovah is a gracious giver.* Her life, too, proved the point.

Joanna was a woman of wealth; she was married to Cuza, the manager of King Herod's household. Life in the king's court had been the order of her day. Yet she was needy. Doctor Luke mentions Joanna two times in his Gospel. First, she is listed among the women whom Jesus had healed or delivered. (The Scriptures never spell out the situation from which Jesus delivered Joanna.)

In response and gratitude for Jesus' gracious gift to her, she followed Him and gave of her own means to support His ministry (Luke 8:1–3). Everywhere Jesus and His disciples went, Joanna and several other women also went. Jesus accepted their heartfelt donations, although in the culture of the day this would have been considered scandalous.[1]

Not only did Joanna give to the Lord who had delivered her, but she listened intently to the words He spoke. When Jesus spoke His parables, Joanna was there. When Jesus pointed to His followers and spoke of them as His mother and brothers because they were doing those things that please His Father (Luke 8:21), He was pointing to Joanna, among others in His circle.

Joanna was a faithful follower, even after Christ's crucifixion. Luke records that Joanna was among the women who rose early Sunday morning to go to His tomb and anoint His body for proper burial. She was there when they discovered that Jesus' body was gone. She bowed to the ground in terror as two blazing angels appeared before her. "The men said to them, 'Why do you look for the living among the dead? He is not here; he has risen! Remember how he told you, while he was still with you in Galilee: "The Son of Man must be delivered into the hands of sinful men, be crucified and on the third day be raised again.'" Then they remembered his words" (Luke 24:5–8).

Of course, Joanna remembered. How could she have forgotten any of the life-giving words Jesus had spoken in her presence? The circumstances began to make sense, in this light. So she and the other women (including Mary Magdalene) ran back to tell the disciples this good news. Joanna believed, although the eleven disciples still doubted.

The evidence of God's hand in our lives may not be as dramatic as the healing Joanna received or the baby Nina and Craig have the opportunity to raise. Yet God is unchangeable; He has no favorites among His children. He offers hand-chosen gifts to each of us, and He wants to pour good things into our laps: "good measure, pressed down, shaken together and running over" (Luke 6:38).

In gratitude for the deliverance she received from the gracious hand of God, Joanna offered back to the Lord her reputation, her loyalty, her unwavering trust, and her lifelong gratitude. The question in our lives is, How will each of us respond to and use the gifts God has given to us?

Lord, I am grateful for the many ways You show me Your grace. I choose to follow You, giving back to You out of the abundance of all You have given me. Amen.

NOTE

1. John F. Walvoord and Roy B. Zuck, *The Bible Knowledge Commentary* (Wheaton, Ill.: Scripture Press, 1985). Article on Luke 8:1–3.

39

SUSANNA:
LILY

> After this, Jesus traveled about from one town and village to another, proclaiming the good news of the kingdom of God. The Twelve were with him, and also some women who had been cured of evil spirits and diseases: . . . Susanna; and many others. These women were helping to support them out of their own means. *(Luke 8:1–3)*

No matter where I live, the house where I spent my early childhood will always be *home* to me. There, my parents spent countless hours cultivating the yard and planting and tending fruit trees, garden vegetables, and a rainbow of flowering plants.

We had peonies and roses, lilacs and pansies. My favorites, though, were the fragrant, delicate lilies of the valley. I favored these perennials because they were among the earliest signs of spring, poking their green noses out of late-season snow carpets, harbingers of warm, playful summers to come. Late one fall we sold that house and moved away. I bemoaned the fact that we didn't dig up a patch of lilies of the valley to take with us.

The following spring, though, Rose, one of my mother's lifelong friends, showed up at our door with an armful of cuttings from her patch of lilies of the valley—cuttings that we could plant in our new yard and enjoy for years to come. Years earlier, Mom had brought Rose a similar gift from our yard, and they had spread out, making their home in her yard. Now she returned the favor. I rejoiced as I stuffed my nose into the perfumed white blossoms. Rose has since moved, and the fragrance of these same lilies again wafts through her new yard each spring.

Lilies of the valley are classified in the *Liliaceae* (lily) family. They are hearty flowers, coming up every year at the same time without fail, regardless of the conditions aboveground. They spread rapidly; in fact, they are contagious in a garden—they'll take over if you let them. All this to say that a lily of the valley is not a bad metaphor for the way Christians should affect the gardens in which we are planted.

Throughout Scripture, members of the *Liliaceae* family are used symbolically. Among all the sacred design elements God gave Solomon for completing the temple, lilies were used to ornament the magnificent pillars. And in Song of Songs, lilies and lilies of the valley describe the pure love of the courting couple (2:1–2; 4:5; 5:13; 6:3).

The connection in New Testament days (and even today) remains unmistakable. In our songs we often refer to Jesus as our "Lily of the Valley." The white lily remains a symbol of purity. Traditionally, the decorative presence of a Madonna lily or a Bermuda lily announces Christ's resurrection in churches around the world on Resurrection Sunday (Easter).

One lily in Scripture is a particularly good example for us to follow: Susanna, whose name means *Lily*. Like Mary Magdalene and Joanna, Susanna had experienced Jesus' healing touch. She, too, followed Christ from town to town, giving financially to support His ministry. She is mentioned only once in Scripture, by Luke (8:1–3). Since Luke mentioned her by name but did not elaborate on Susanna's healing or on her character, we can deduce that she may have been well known to his audience—probably as a continued faithful follower of Christ in the years following the Master's crucifixion, resurrection, and ascension.

It's likely also that Susanna was in Christ's audience the day He was discussing anxiety with the crowd. I can picture her listening attentively as He sought an example of worry-less living that the crowd could easily understand. "Consider," He said, "consider how the lilies grow. They do not labor or spin. Yet I tell you, not even Solomon in all his splendor was dressed like one of these" (Luke 12:27). Then He explained it to the crowd: "So don't worry about tomorrow; God will handle your tomorrow" (v. 28, my paraphrase).

Yes, Susanna would have understood. There had been a day when she worried about tomorrow, but that was before Jesus brought her a personal miracle. Now life was different for her. She served a Master who loved her, a God who reached down and touched her, and she knew there was nothing left to worry about.

Maybe we should take Jesus' words literally. Maybe we should consider *this* lily.

As with countless others whom Jesus touched, Susanna received a cleansing from *Immanuel: God with us*. She now wore her name with greater worthiness, because she had become a pure, loyal vessel in active use for God's grand purposes, a beautiful flower crafted and recrafted by the loving hand of God.

She must have been a woman with some money at her disposal, because Luke records that she was helping support the ministry out of her "own means" (8:3). Her giving came out of a willing, grateful heart. That leads to a marvelous principle: those who share in Christ's ministry also share in its rewards. "And if anyone gives even a cup of cold water to one of these little ones because he is my disciple, I tell you the truth, he will certainly not lose his reward" (Matthew 10:42).

There is awaiting Susanna (and all of us who are Christ's pure lilies) a heavenly prize—the reward of eternal joy, eternal celebration, eternal life in the presence of the Master she followed faithfully on earth.

Jesus, You have made such a difference in my life, and I want to thank You in a tangible way. I want to give myself away for You, to serve You by serving Your people, to enhance Your reputation by building up Your ministry. Thank You for the privilege of giving back to You. Amen.

40

TABITHA:
A FEMALE GAZELLE

In Joppa there was a disciple named Tabitha
(which, when translated, is Dorcas), who was
always doing good and helping the poor. (*Acts
9:36*)

On September 5, 1997, an eighty-seven-year-old
Catholic nun died on her bed in India; her
heart simply gave out. Known to the world as
Mother Teresa of Calcutta, this woman spent more
than forty-five years caring for the destitute, lowest
caste outcasts in Calcutta's teeming, stinking, filthy
streets. To minister to these forgotten people, she
set up a hospice, a leper colony, and a nursery for
abandoned children, and she established similar
ministries in 105 more countries.

International leaders recognized her accomplishments by heaping upon her numerous well-
publicized honors, including the Nobel Peace Prize
(in 1979). But Mother Teresa did not work for human rewards; she worked because she loved. "The
poor must know we love them," she said. "The poor
do not need our sympathy and pity. They need our
love and compassion." Her response to receiving
the Nobel Prize was, "I am not worthy. I am nothing but a pencil in God's hands."

The first question on everyone's lips when the
world learned of Mother Teresa's death was, "Who
will pick up the mantle now?" Certainly, thousands

of other nuns, priests, and lay workers participated in the ministries Mother Teresa spearheaded, but it was she who had the intense passion to serve the poor; it was she who provided the impetus for ministry. Who would infuse in others a love for the unlovely now that she was gone?

Mother Teresa was the modern-day counterpart of women down through the ages who have given of themselves to serve the poor. Tabitha—*a female gazelle* (also known by her name's Greek equivalent, Dorcas)—gave her life away in the same attitude of service in New Testament times.

Tabitha became an early convert to Christianity, perhaps as a result of Philip the evangelist's ministry in Joppa (a trading port city on the Mediterranean Sea, about thirty-five miles northwest of Jerusalem). After her conversion, Tabitha worked to become like Christ in every aspect of life. Like Peter, James, John, and the others, Scripture calls Tabitha not just a believer, but a *disciple* (Acts 9:36).

She took to heart Jesus' words in Matthew 25:35–36, "For I was hungry and you gave me something to eat, I was thirsty and you gave me something to drink, I was a stranger and you invited me in, I needed clothes and you clothed me, I was sick and you looked after me, I was in prison and you came to visit me." Probably a woman of some means in Joppa, the disciple Tabitha cared for the poor, providing them clothes, food, all the necessities—always (according to Acts 9:36).

I wonder if Tabitha came to Paul's mind as he wrote, "For we are God's workmanship, created in Christ Jesus to do good works, which God prepared in advance for us to do" (Ephesians 2:10) or when he wrote that women should be clothed "with good deeds, appropriate for women who profess to worship God" (1 Timothy 2:9–10).

Then Tabitha became ill and died. All the widows she served grieved, wondering who would care for them with Tabitha gone. They sent for Peter, who was ministering in the neighboring town of Lydda.

Peter came quickly, while the woman's body was still lying in an upstairs room of her home. He watched and listened as "all the widows stood around him, crying and showing him the robes and other clothing that Dorcas had made while she was still with them" (Acts 9:39). Sending everyone out of her room, Peter got down on his knees and prayed. He got alone with God. He would not make it a public spectacle if God chose to perform a miracle.

As a result of that prayer, Peter turned to the dead body and said, "Tabitha, arise" (Acts 9:40 NKJV). His words were reminiscent of his Master's words to the little daughter of Jairus, the synagogue ruler. Jesus had told her, "Little girl, arise" (Luke 8:54 NKJV). The Greek words were different, but the meaning was the same—as was the result. Tabitha, like Jairus's daughter, was raised to life again.

Peter presented her to the believers and the widows, and they were so overjoyed that they spread the word everywhere. "This became known all over Joppa, and many people believed in the Lord" (Acts 9:42). God used this miracle to bring many souls into His fold and to restore (for a time) a woman whose continuous good deeds to the poor spoke well of His kingdom.

I keep coming back to the word that described how often Tabitha did her good deeds: ALWAYS. The testimony of the lives of Tabitha and of Mother Teresa precipitates in me—as it probably should in each of us—a self-evaluation. What is it that we do for the good of God's kingdom—always—even when no one is looking and when we don't feel like it?

Dear Lord, may I always do the work of ministry to which You have called me. Not just when I feel like it, but always and in all ways. Amen.

LYDIA:
TRAVAIL

One of those listening was a woman named Lydia, a dealer in purple cloth from the city of Thyatira, who was a worshiper of God. The Lord opened her heart to respond to Paul's message. *(Acts 16:14)*

Her name was Lucia. She was a tiny woman, but strong, tenacious, industrious.

During depression and war years, Lucia raised six sons and one daughter (a second daughter died as a toddler). Her husband was a missionary, frequently traveling inside the United States and also to Italy to plant the seed of the gospel. Meanwhile Lucia worked in her own grocery store and minded their home. In the Great Depression Lucia's family lost their store, and she then confined her work to her home.

Her working implements were primitive—they required woman-power rather than electricity. To do laundry for her large household, she stood over the sink and cranked each garment through a hand-operated wringer. To iron she fueled her kitchen stove (with oil carried from the cellar) and fired it up so the cumbersome iron could be warmed over its flame.

Lucia carried pounds of groceries down the street as she trudged to her home. She had no microwave conveniences, no prepared frozen foods; Lucia didn't have a bread machine or a box of

Prince spaghetti. Every lump of dough she plied by hand. She even hung drying spaghetti from racks lining the halls and bedrooms of her apartment.

All day, Lucia could be heard singing hymns and gospel songs. She was not just whistling while she worked, but praising the Lord while she lovingly travailed for her family. And every night that the church doors were open, Lucia was present, joyfully praising her Savior.

Lucia was my great-grandmother. I can hardly imagine the strength required for her labors—yet she did not complain. Here I sit perched in a comfortable chair in a comfortably warm, well-lit room, moving only my fingers as words appear on a computer screen as quickly as I can think them. This is what *I* call hard work. I complain about lifting a Tupperware container of prepared food into the microwave; my complaining quotient would reach an all-time peak if I were transported into Lucia's world.

Thinking about the many stories of Lucia's life brought to mind the Proverbs 31 woman, who is seen hard at work from predawn to postdusk. She buys and works a field (works outside the home), makes fabric (works inside the home), rises early to prepare food for her household (serves her family), enhances her husband's reputation (serves her husband), and obediently follows God (serves the Lord). Her example seems unattainable to me, yet many women down through the centuries have come close to achieving it.

One such woman appears briefly in the book of Acts. Her name is Lydia, *travail*. A resident of Philippi (in Greece) during the time of the apostle

Paul's missionary journeys, Lydia was originally
from Thyatira (in Asia). She was a businesswoman
of some means; she traded in purple dyes (perhaps
purple fabric) that were highly valued. Thyatira
was known as a center of purple production, and
the purple trade was important to Philippi's econo-
my. There was Lydia, in the center of it all.

Lydia has much to teach modern-day business-
women. She was a worshiper of God, probably a
convert to Judaism. She set aside time in her busy
schedule for God. On the Sabbath Paul and his
companions found Lydia on a riverbank worshiping God with other women. As Paul spoke of Jesus,
His atoning death and resurrection, Lydia's heart
quickened. She recognized the truth in Paul's words
and believed. And so Lydia became the first recorded convert to Christianity in all of Europe.

Lydia's enthusiasm must have been contagious,
as her household was converted at her testimony
and baptized into the faith. Then she begged Paul
and his company, "If you consider me a believer in
the Lord, come and stay at my house" (Acts 16:15).

Her home became the center of their teaching
ministry in Philippi. It was on their way to worship
in her home that Paul and Silas met a slave girl with
an evil spirit. After days of the girl following them
and shouting at them, Paul commanded the spirit
to come out of her in Jesus' name. This infuriated
her owners, who made money from her fortune-
telling; soon the missionaries were beaten and
jailed. But while the two were praising God at mid-
night, an earthquake shook the jail and loosed the
prisoners' chains. The jailer was converted; Paul
and Silas were released. Before leaving Philippi the

two returned to Lydia's home to encourage the believers.

I am in awe of Lydia; she was the epitome of everything I'd like to be as a twenty-first-century woman, although she lived in the first century. She ran a successful business, kept a bustling household in line, and didn't miss a beat in maintaining her faith and worship. Her heart was pliable and open; she acted quickly and decisively once she was convinced of the gospel's truth.

Lydia's workload would have been heavy enough without inviting long-term houseguests and a growing congregation of believers into her home. For Lydia's working implements were to Lucia's as Lucia's are to mine. Lucia's conveniences would seem miraculous and extravagant to a first-century homemaker. Yet she didn't hesitate to make the invitation, didn't consider the labor cost excessive. She begged Paul and Silas to honor her home with their presence. She would have been deeply offended had they refused.

"Who can find a virtuous woman? for her price is far above rubies" asks Proverbs 31:10 (KJV). Like rubies, the worker's value is high. Lydia. Lucia. And countless women like them. Their travail at home and abroad has brought much good fruit to the kingdom of God.

Father, I want to work willingly and graciously for You as have the many godly women who have gone before. Teach me to be virtuous, as they were. Amen.

42

DAMARIS:
GENTLE

A few men became followers of Paul and believed. Among them was Dionysius, a member of the Areopagus, also a woman named Damaris, and a number of others. *(Acts 17:34)*

Most Christian colleges require all students to take two courses on the Bible: Old Testament Survey and New Testament Survey. Most students dutifully sign the form saying they've read the entire testament during the term and continue on their way, virtually unchanged as a result of a quick pass over the Scriptures.

My experience was different. My professor for New Testament Survey harped over and over on one point. I don't remember any session when he didn't admonish us to do as the Berean believers had done: to go home and search the Scriptures for ourselves, to see whether what he was telling us was true (Acts 17:11).

This professor did more than provide his students with a quick overview of what is in the Bible. Instead, he poured into us a deep need to know for ourselves what Scripture says, so we will not be deceived by false doctrine. He taught us to think clearly, to work hard to discern the difference between truth and falsehood. He equipped us to recognize God's Word when we heard it proclaimed truthfully.

There is a woman, mentioned by name in Scripture only once, to whom God revealed Himself as a result of a thoughtful presentation of His truth. Her name was Damaris, *gentle*.

Damaris was a resident of Athens who spent at least some of her time on Mars Hill, the place about which Scripture says, "All the Athenians and the foreigners who lived there spent their time doing nothing but talking about and listening to the latest ideas" (Acts 17:21). Because of her presence there, we can surmise that Damaris was a thinker. She was inquisitive. She was attentive.

Damaris was on Mars Hill the day a new thinker took his message to the crowd. The apostle Paul, acknowledging his hearers' "religiosity," began by saying: "I see that in every way you are very religious. For as I walked around and looked carefully at your objects of worship, I even found an altar with this inscription: TO AN UNKNOWN GOD. Now what you worship as something unknown I am going to proclaim to you" (Acts 17:22–23).

Thus began one of the most succinct yet well-reasoned presentations of the gospel recorded in Scripture. After hearing the truth proclaimed, some in the crowd sneered at Paul, others (while not yet convinced) asked to hear him again, but only a handful chose to believe. Two are named: Dionysius (a member of the council) and the woman Damaris.

I'd like to think that part of the reason for Damaris's openness can be found in a study of the character quality described by her name. *Gentle*. What wild animal is gentle? They must be tamed, curbed, restrained. Likewise, gentleness is not inherent in our natures.

Gentleness is a concept integrally woven through the New Testament. It is listed as a fruit of the Spirit (Galatians 5:22–23), it is a quality demonstrated by Jesus Himself (2 Corinthians 10:1), and it is a command for believers. Listen to Paul's closing admonition to the Philippians in verse 5 of chapter 4: "Let your gentleness be evident to all." Why? Because "The Lord is near."

Somehow, Dionysius and Damaris were able to discern the truth from among the various philosophies they heard regularly debated on Mars Hill. Perhaps they recognized a gentleness and meekness in the apostle Paul. Perhaps something else drew them.

Not knowing any other facts about these two, we can only assume the Spirit of God quickened their hearts and made them receptive to the message. They were searchers for truth, and God promises to reward those who "diligently seek him" (Hebrews 11:6 KJV).

What was it about Paul's message that attracted these thinkers? Certainly Paul made his message relevant to issues that concerned them. His preamble acknowledged their own search, and he even quoted their own poets (Acts 17:28). One phrase that stands out is in verse 27, where Paul explains why God made each person and established a unique plan for everyone: "God did this so that men would seek him and perhaps reach out for him and find him, though he is not far from each one of us."

This truth would resonate in Damaris's heart, fulfilling her quest for purpose in a way no other philosophy ever could. God created her so she could find Him. It was a truth that gripped her soul and wouldn't let her leave without deciding to reach out to God. We know the moment we reach out for God, He will allow us to find Him.

Perhaps the Scriptures mention Damaris because she was decisive: She was persuaded, and she believed. She didn't wait and contemplate what she'd heard until her slow action became an excuse for a lack of action. She began to follow Paul immediately, listening and learning about this unknown God who was now becoming known to her.

We are not so unlike Damaris. Our culture is filled with "new" ideas and philosophies debated on our Mars Hills—in the media, at the lunch table, during a civic meeting. Damaris had the apostle Paul to explain the truth to her; we have something even better: God's inspired Word—our one-stop source for ultimate truth. Without an intimate knowledge of His Word, though, we could never expect to discern the difference between truth and deception in our mixed-up culture.

My Lord, enable me to mine the depths of Your Word with the insight that comes from You. Equip me to discern between truth and error in all I encounter. Amen.

43

PRISCILLA:
ANCIENT

Greet Priscilla and Aquila, my fellow
workers in Christ Jesus. They risked their lives
for me. Not only I but all the churches of the
Gentiles are grateful to them. *(Romans 16:3–4)*

Several months ago, I was sitting in a hospital
waiting room on a Friday evening nervously
awaiting word on the progress of my mother's
emergency surgery. The TV was blaring, and it
served its purpose—to temporarily distract me
from my worry. Across its screen paraded valuable
antiques—vases, furniture, Civil War memorabilia,
and the like. It turned out we were watching a PBS
series on antique appraising.

What surprised me was that the objects were
more valuable if they had not been restored by
modern hands. A fresh coat of varnish, a repair to a
broken chair leg, a sanding of the rough spots
would diminish the item's value exponentially. An
armoire that would have been worth $10,000 in its
original state could in a restored condition bring
only a few hundred dollars.

This seemed especially odd to my modern
mind-set. We work tirelessly at making ourselves
look younger and smoother and fresher rather than
worn or tired or crinkled. I find it odd that young-
looking, refurbished people would most value
*un*refurbished objects.

This dichotomy came to mind as I studied what we know of the life of one pillar in the New Testament church, a woman named Priscilla—which means *ancient*. I looked up *ancient* in Webster's dictionary; one of its synonyms is *venerable*. So I looked up *venerable*. Among other things its definition says: "made sacred" and "calling forth respect through age, character, and attainments." Priscilla was more than an ancient character from the olden days. Her story doesn't need a fresh coat of varnish to make her lessons relevant to us.

Priscilla (also called Prisca) was a Jewish woman married to a Jewish man, Aquila; together they made their living in the trade of tentmaking. For years they lived in Rome, but one day the capricious Claudius ordered all Jews out of Rome. The couple packed up their gear and moved on. They landed in the port city of Corinth, Greece's most important trade center—and also a center of prostitution (male and female), gambling, and other debauchery. It was God's providence that they chose Corinth, because shortly after they arrived another Jewish traveler came to the city—the apostle Paul.

Because Paul, too, was a tentmaker, the couple and the apostle quickly became friends. They accepted the gospel message and invited Paul to live and work with them. As Paul preached and reasoned with the Jews and the Greeks, he offended many (as the message of the gospel always will), making him unpopular with the angry crowds. Yet Priscilla and Aquila stood by him during his year and a half of ministry in Corinth, harboring him in their home at the risk of their lives.

Since their roots were shallow in Corinth, Priscilla and Aquila shipped out to Ephesus when the apostle did. Their faith was deep enough that Paul soon was able to leave the couple to minister for Christ in Ephesus while he continued his missionary journey to Caesarea and Antioch.

In the synagogue of Ephesus, the couple heard a bold new preacher, Apollos, who had a "thorough knowledge of the Scriptures" (Acts 18:24) and who "taught about Jesus accurately" (v. 25), but who knew nothing beyond John's baptism. Priscilla and Aquila invited him into their home and taught him the salvation of Christ, discipling him and equipping him with the true message. He then went out and led many to Christ.

Paul always gratefully remembered the sacrifices and dangers his friends Priscilla and Aquila had made for him. They had been living embodiments of Christ's love, putting their lives on the line for him. Remember Jesus' words, "Greater love has no one than this, that he lay down his life for his friends" (John 15:13).

Paul mentioned the couple lovingly in several of his letters to the churches, always referring to both husband and wife as partners in the ministry —co-laborers, equals with him. There is some speculation that the mysterious writer of the book of Hebrews could have been Priscilla and her husband, Aquila.

I wish I knew more about Priscilla. She must have been educated, because she and her husband together explained the good news of salvation to the learned Apollos. What would she have felt, being displaced from her Roman home and embarking on a dangerous journey to a notorious city? What was going through her mind as she set up housekeeping and a business with no friends, no family but her husband nearby? She must have been glad when her husband brought Paul home—a kindred spirit who was carrying the message of life. It would have been instinctive for her to protect this friend when the fickle crowd turned against him. Did her heart quicken at the thought of leaving Corinth for a ministry in Ephesus?

Priscilla, *ancient*? Maybe—in the *venerable* sense of the word. Her life was an example of one who was faithful to the sometimes-dangerous, always-adventurous call God placed on her life; she was one "made sacred" by her association with the work of Jesus Christ. And yes, in many ways, she deserves to be respected down through the ages for her "character and attainments." For she lived an example of godliness that led others to the Savior. That is the eternally priceless value of this woman of antiquity.

Lord, looking at Priscilla's life has made me won-der what I've ever done that would make other believers grateful for my ministry as Paul was for hers. Equip me to live in such a way that I bless and minister to Your people each day. Amen.

44

PHOEBE:
RADIANT

I commend to you our sister Phoebe, a servant of the church in Cenchrea. I ask you to receive her in the Lord in a way worthy of the saints and to give her any help she may need from you, for she has been a great help to many people, including me. *(Romans 16:1–2)*

As a child, I devoured novels, especially those written by Louisa May Alcott. In *Eight Cousins* Alcott paints a picture of two girls whose lives intersect; the author chronicles their growing friendship. These two girls, Rose and Phebe, have stayed with me into adulthood.

The stark contrasts between the two could not be more pronounced. Rose was dressed in costly frocks; she was an orphan, but doted over by aunts and cousins alike. Her hand-clothed doll collection would make even twentieth-century girls green with envy. Phebe, though, was dressed in rags, elbow-deep in dirty, sudsy water, an orphan who had to do kitchen labor for her keep. Rose spent her days aimlessly wandering the mansion, awash in tears and wallowing in heartache. Phebe amused herself as she scrubbed the kitchen by chirping all sorts of birdcalls; she literally whistled while she worked. Phebe's sunny personality soon drew out the sullen Rose, her cheery disposition doing immeasurably more for the grieving girl than all the medicine Rose's aunts could afford.

Alcott's Phebe embodies the true character of her name, which in the Greek means *radiant*.

In Romans 16:1–2 the apostle Paul introduces Christians of all time to his Corinthian sister in Christ, Phoebe (spelled "Phebe" in King James English), another aptly named woman whose countenance reflects the radiance of one who joyfully serves others.

The bustling trade city of Corinth was known for its debauchery; it was a seat of pagan idolatry, a moral vacuum. In Corinth, as in our metropolitan world, the ugly sludge of darkness oozed into every corner. People reveled in their filthy practices, blinded to the fact that they were stuck in a muck that would destroy them.

About A.D. 51, during his second missionary journey, Paul established a thriving church in Corinth. Cenchrea, a port town located about seven miles east of the city of Corinth, was home to Phoebe and the church she served as deaconess.

In Christian tradition, the office of deaconess carried with it the same qualifications as those for deacons. In the early centuries, a deaconess taught the faith to women converts, ministered to women who were ill or imprisoned, anointed and baptized women. Phoebe probably performed many of these tasks.

As Paul lovingly referred to Phoebe as "our sister" in this letter to the Romans, he was calling to the Roman believers' minds Jesus' words recorded in Matthew 12:50: "For whoever does the will of my Father in heaven is my brother and sister and mother."

Although the details of this sister's life remain

largely hidden to us, her character traits are on record for all to see. She was a woman of service who put the needs of others ahead of her own. She gave of herself unselfishly to assist Paul in his ministry. She was a participant in ministry—active, not passive.

Commentators draw many conclusions from the respectful words the apostle Paul used to commend this woman to the Roman believers. The text implies that Phoebe was a woman of means, perhaps a widow, who opened her home to the early church for meetings, who entertained Paul and the other visiting missionaries.

Many believe it was Phoebe whom Paul entrusted to deliver his epistle to the Roman church. This woman was traveling to Rome and would arrive alone, a stranger in a foreign country. Perhaps she had business in the city. Or maybe her business was simply to deliver Paul's letter. Yet since Phoebe was a sister in Christ, Paul's words of high commendation—much like a letter of reference in our day—asked the Roman believers to show her kindness and tender care with the same measure she used to care for the Cenchrean believers.

The Greek root word for Phoebe's name (*phos-*) carries with it the connotation that light has a subtle, delicate, brilliant quality, and that it cannot help but be exposed to the view of all. Similarly, this godly woman's delicate but brilliant beacon invaded the abject darkness of metropolitan Corinth and shone brightly, declaring that in love her Savior was seeking those lost in sin.

Jesus, ever aware of the works of darkness, called his followers to "let your light shine before men, that they may see your good deeds and praise your Father in heaven" (Matthew 5:16). He calls us to be that radiant light shining before the men and women in the towns and cities where our Lord has called us to serve. He calls us to serve cheerfully, in the same spirit in which Alcott's Phebe approached her labors and Paul's friend Phoebe approached hers.

Dear Lord Jesus, please equip me with the attitude of Phoebe as I serve Your church. May I be a radiant example of Your love to this world, whose light seems to be fading so quickly. Amen.

45

LOIS:
AGREEABLE

> I have been reminded of your sincere faith,
> which first lived in your grandmother Lois and
> in your mother Eunice and, I am persuaded,
> now lives in you also. (2 Timothy 1:5)

College students live to receive mail from home. Today, it's a synthetic voice on e-mail announcing, "You've got mail." In days gone by it was a full metal cube at the campus post office. I remember the exhilaration of going to the CPO to find even last week's church bulletin from home with a note scribbled on it.

By far my favorite mail from home came from my grandmother and grandfather. Periodically, they would buy a pretty card, each jot a short note, and enclose a twenty-dollar bill to be spent on "anything I wanted." Usually, it financed an overdue sitting under the hair stylist's scissors. The cards were too nice to throw away, so I stashed them in a file folder.

One day, six or eight years later, I was cleaning files. Coming across those cards, I began to read them again. In the interim, Papa had gone to be with Jesus. I noticed that on each card he had written out the address to a Scripture passage under his signature. I had never taken the time to look them up. But that day, I did. In them, I found a rich heritage that Papa left behind especially for me, his only grandchild. Through the Scriptures he chose, he had been telling me he was proud of me, he wanted me to keep serving the Lord, and he knew he had fulfilled God's plan for his life. Papa left me a legacy of Scriptures.

This is a legacy that young pastor Timothy received from his grandmother, Lois, according to 2 Timothy 1:5.

Lois was the first believer in Christ in her family. She passed along to her daughter Eunice and to her grandson Timothy a sincere faith. To have had such a powerful impact on her loved ones—those who knew her actions every day—she must have fit the key quality evident in her name, *agreeable*. Webster's dictionary describes this quality as "being in harmony" and "pleasing to the mind or senses." She must have been a virtuous woman, pleasing to be around, a harmonious woman to emulate.

Because of her sincere faith, the apostle Paul had taken notice of Lois. In his commentary, Matthew Henry notes about Lois and her daughter Eunice: "Paul speaks of them both with great respect, as women of eminent virtue and piety, and commends them especially for their unfeigned faith [2 Timothy 1:5], their sincerity embracing and adhering to the doctrine of Christ."[1]

Sincerity is a theme that comes through in many of the writings of the apostles. Unfeigned, truthful, down-deep-rooted faith in Jesus Christ. These are important qualities in the life of true believers. Peter commands his hearers to "have sincere love for your brothers" (1 Peter 1:22)— translation: don't fake it, mean it! James talks of heavenly wisdom as being "first of all pure; then peace-loving, considerate, submissive, full of mercy and good fruit, impartial and sincere" (James 3:17). Paul writes that godly love comes from "a pure heart and a good conscience and a sincere faith" (1 Timothy 1:5).

Even today, our sincerity and our agreeability —if founded on the truth of faith in Jesus Christ— will set us apart from everyone else in the world. If we display these qualities, perhaps the "good fruit" we bear will be like the fruit Lois bore and the fruit my grandparents bore. Our families will be won to the faith—and so will many others who touch our lives.

God, teach me to love You with all my heart. In every way, may I be sincerely Yours. Amen.

NOTE

1. Acts 16:1–5 from Matthew Henry's Commentary on the Whole Bible: New Modern Edition database © 1991, 1994 by Hendrickson Publishers, Inc.

46

EUNICE:
GOOD VICTORY

> He came to Derbe and then to Lystra, where
> a disciple named Timothy lived, whose mother
> was a Jewess and a believer, but whose father
> was a Greek. (*Acts 16:1*)

My earliest memories are of sitting in my high
chair beside the kitchen table and listening to
my mother read Bible stories to me. First, she'd feed
me breakfast. Then she'd feed me Scriptures. I was
just an infant when she began this daily routine.

It wasn't a picture book, but she made it both
entertaining and educational. Her vocal inflections
changed as she read of the different characters.
When I got older and began to ask questions, she
patiently answered me.

I guess I always knew my parents read the
Scriptures together and prayed every night. But
most often when they read together, I'd be long
since asleep after a busy day of playing with my little friends and my toys. On Sunday nights, though,
church lasted until 9:30, getting us home near 10
P.M. So, on those nights my parents would tuck me
in and read the Scriptures in quick succession.

One night when I was about two-and-a-half,
Daddy was reading to Mama about young Samuel,
unaware that I was awake and listening. When he
got to the part where the voice of God calls out during the night, "Samuel, Saaaaamuel . . ." I promptly

responded, "What do you want?" That brought peals of laughter from my parents' room.

Children listen, and they understand more than we know. This is a truth that one Bible mother used to great advantage. Her name was Eunice, which means *a good victory* or *happily conquering.* You may not recognize her name, but you'll surely remember her son, Timothy—the young pastor discipled in later years by the apostle Paul. Eunice's happy victory was that from Timothy's infancy she taught him the Scriptures (2 Timothy 3:15) and, in adulthood, he chose to live his life in accordance with what she had taught.

The daughter of another godly woman (Lois), Eunice was married to a Greek man. We have no indication that he was a believer in Jesus Christ. The family lived in Lystra in the hill country of what is modern-day Turkey. It was in Lystra that Paul and Barnabas were at first hailed as gods (after healing a crippled man) and then stoned by the disillusioned multitude. Certainly this was not an easy place to be a believer.

Eunice named her son *God-honorer,* and that is what he would one day become. According to Paul's testimony, Eunice taught Timothy by word and example, even in the imperfect circumstance of a marriage where her husband probably was not a believer. She nurtured and discipled this young man toward a sincere faith (2 Timothy 1:5), and he came to be a worthy associate of God's chosen apostles, elders, and preachers. Only God knows how many people were won to Christ and how many people were discipled in the truth as a result of Eunice's son's ministry.

Through his mother, Timothy came to love the Word of God. In his day that encompassed only what we now know as the Old Testament.

Since my mother made Bible reading a joyful occasion, I remember the joy of beginning to read the Bible back to my mother. Haltingly I sounded out the words and made sense of the letters that presented themselves on the page. Soon, I was practicing reading the Bible out loud on my own.

At that time, my grandfather (our pastor) had been ill for many months and had not slept more than a few snatches during the entire ordeal. One day when I was nearly five, I brought my Bible into his room. Proud of my accomplishment, I began to read a psalm aloud to him. As I finished, I looked up only to see that he had fallen asleep on me. Crestfallen, I ran into the living room, crying to my mother, "Papa fell asleep on me." After a quick hug, she explained that God had used my reading to help Papa rest. While I don't recommend falling asleep while listening to the Scriptures as a general course, my mother used this situation to teach me another aspect of God's loving character—that His Word is powerful and very much alive today.

This lesson is similar to one Eunice passed along to her son Timothy. It's a lesson Paul mentioned later in Timothy's life:

> But as for you, continue in what you have learned and have become convinced of, because you know those from whom you learned it, and how from infancy you have known the holy Scriptures, which are able to make you wise for salvation through faith in Christ Jesus. All Scripture is God-breathed and is useful for teaching, re-

*buking, correcting and training in righteousness, so that
the man of God may be thoroughly equipped for every
good work. (2 Timothy 3:14–17)*

Although no one can inherit faith in Christ, a
mother like Eunice—a mother like mine—can lead
the way for her child to love God and to hunger for
His Word.

*God, establish within my heart a love for Your
Word and an insatiable desire to teach others to love
You and Your Holy Scriptures. Amen.*

47

WIFE:
A FRUITFUL VINE

> A wife of noble character who can find? She
> is worth far more than rubies. Her husband has
> full confidence in her and lacks nothing of
> value. She brings him good, not harm, all the
> days of her life. (*Proverbs 31:10–12*)

From the time I could barely toddle across the
grass and plant myself at the foot of an apple
tree, our family has made an annual autumn pil-
grimage to Michigan or Wisconsin to pick apples.

Some of my favorite memories are of "climb-
ing" apple trees with my friends and perching
between the V-shaped branches (no more than
three feet off the ground) clutching a half-eaten apple in each sticky fist. I remember the delicious
fragrance of juicy apples accosting us before we
even drove into the orchard. Nothing could be
more heavenly than picking ripe fruit from its
branch and sinking my teeth into its tender flesh.

This year's apple excursion wasn't nearly so
fruitful, though. After a summer of mild temperatures and little sustained precipitation (although we
did experience a few flash floods), the bright red
fruit that looked delicious from afar was actually
dry, tasteless, tough-skinned. Our anticipation
dashed, we drove home with an empty trunk where
a bushel of apples should have been bobbling and
rolling from every nook and cranny. The orchard
didn't even have homemade cider to sell; our

thirsty family had to stop at McDonald's on the way home to whet our dry mouths with Diet Coke, a poor replacement for fresh cider.

Fruit is a common theme in Scriptures. It is as old as the Garden of Eden—in fact, it was a bite into forbidden fruit that got the world off to a really bad start.

Listen to Jesus' metaphor: "Every good tree bears good fruit, but a bad tree bears bad fruit. A good tree cannot bear bad fruit, nor can a bad tree bear good fruit. Every tree that does not bear good fruit is cut down and thrown into the fire. Therefore by their fruits you will know them" (Matthew 7:17–20 NKJV). Likewise, evidence of God's Spirit at work within believers is called the "fruit of the Spirit." That is: "love, joy, peace, patience, kindness, goodness, faithfulness, gentleness and self-control" (Galatians 5:22–23).

The Old Testament offers metaphors for a godly wife: she is more valuable than rubies (Proverbs 31:10); she is like "a fruitful vine" (Psalm 128:3). The writer of Proverbs offers equally telling pictures of a not-so-godly wife: "A wife of noble character is her husband's crown, but a disgraceful wife is like decay in his bones" (12:4); "A quarrelsome wife is like a constant dripping on a rainy day" (27:15). Ouch!

One wife we are quick to throw into that second category is a woman we know only as Job's wife. She has but one line in Scripture, and it's a doozy. She tells her pained husband, "Are you still holding on to your integrity? Curse God and die!" (Job 2:9).

Job's wife doesn't qualify for the Proverbs 31

award for wifely virtue, at least not at this moment of her life. But let's step back and look at her situation more closely.

This wife was used to enjoying nothing but the best of God's blessings. She had it all: a house filled with healthy children; an abundance of food and clothing; more worldly wealth than any of her contemporaries; and a God-fearing husband of impeccable character. Then in one swoosh of the devil's brush, her world collapsed: her children were killed, their property was destroyed, and her once-vigorous husband was reduced to a diseased heap of depressed, dejected humanity.

We'd all like to think we would have pulled up an ash heap next to husband Job, put on our own potato-sack garment, and administered salve to his sores. Maybe some of us would respond that way. But it is as likely (perhaps more so) that we would sink into our own depression and begin thinking: "What's the use of serving God? How could He do this to the man I love? Job has been faithful to God, and what has it gotten him? What has it gotten our family?" Wallowing in this line of thought turned Job's wife toward the sinful path where she turned her back on God.

There is an implication in Job's response to his wife that she had a history of godliness: "You are talking like a foolish woman [not you *are* a foolish woman, but you're *talking like* one]. Shall we accept good from God, and not trouble?" (Job 2:10).

We never see whether Job's wife turned back to God and found comfort in His arms. We do know that when Job's fortunes were restored in chapter 42, his wife would have shared the blessing, said to be greater than anything taken away (v. 12). Since God gave Job seven new sons and three new daughters (v. 13), one could easily infer that Job's wife was their mother.

Contrary to his culture, Job valued his daughters as equals with his sons. He "granted them an inheritance along with their brothers" (42:15). While the Scriptures do not record the names of the seven sons, we do know the names Job chose for his daughters: Jemimah (an affectionate term for *dove*), Keziah (*cassia*, a spice similar to cinnamon), and Keren-Happuch (*a flask of cosmetic*, whose root is translated elsewhere as *fair colors*).

From studying Job's wife we gain a reminder of God's mercy. She sinned, yet God restored all that had been taken away. Her husband recovered from his illness and her womb was fruitful once again—bearing ten new children, beautiful children (42:15) given from the gracious hand of a loving God.

"Blessed are all who fear the Lord, who walk in his ways. You will eat the fruit of your labor; blessings and prosperity will be yours. Your wife will be like a fruitful vine within your house; your sons will be like olive shoots around your table. Thus is the man blessed who fears the Lord" (Psalm 128:1–4).

Jesus, let me be a servant of Yours, who brings "good, not harm" to all those in my family, no matter what difficulties You choose to allow in my life. Amen.

48

WIDOW:
A DESOLATE PLACE

Then the word of the Lord came to him: "Go at once to Zarephath of Sidon and stay there. I have commanded a widow in that place to supply you with food." *(1 Kings 17:8–9)*

Journalist Jon Krakauer fulfilled his childhood dream. He climbed to the top of the world—he made it to the top of Mount Everest, and he lived to tell about it. What he found on that peak, though, was anything but the exhilaration of success.

In a September 1996 article in *Outside* magazine, Krakauer chronicled the final stage of his May 1996 ascent this way: "Surrounding me on the plateau were some three dozen people, huddled in tents pitched side by side. Yet an odd sense of isolation hung over the camp. Up here, in this god-forsaken place, I felt distressingly disconnected from everyone around me—emotionally, spiritually, physically. . . . Although we would leave camp in a few hours as a group, we would ascend as individuals, linked to one another by neither rope nor any deep sense of loyalty."

Krakauer's feelings of isolation were forebodings of a greater loss; before that day was over several of his comrades (with whom he had lived for months in preparation for that final ascent) would lose their lives in a terrifying mountain blizzard. One of the last on the peak that night was a

South African man, Herrod. Krakauer notes this dismal thought about the last moments of Herrod's life: "With darkness fast approaching, he was out of oxygen, physically drained, and completely alone on the roof of the world."

Most of us have experienced something akin to what Krakauer describes as "completely alone on the roof of the world" (albeit while nearer to sea level). The words capture that isolated feeling of being abandoned in a fiercely desolate environment, with no one to count on, no one to turn to. Interesting that Krakauer would use the phrase "godforsaken" to describe a well-peopled camp high up on the mountain. For many of us, those desolate times of life leave us feeling forsaken by everyone, especially by God. And yet for those who believe in His name, God has promised, "I will never leave you nor forsake you" (Hebrews 13:5 NKJV).

God seems to have a special place in His heart for one special group of otherwise-forsaken people —widows. The Hebrew roots of the word translated "widow" speak of *a desolate place*. Yet, over and over again God intervenes in the lives of widows to meet their physical needs and to fulfill their spiritual yearnings. After all, Anna (see chapter 9) spent her widowed decades praying in the temple; and it was in the temple courts that she came to meet the everlasting God in the form of the newborn Jesus.

God understands the special challenges of widowhood. He made provision in both Testaments for their care. He directed the Israelites: "When you harvest the grapes in your vineyard, do not go over the vines again. Leave what remains for the alien, the fatherless and the widow" (Deuteronomy

24:21). In the early church, God arranged that several disciples who were full of the Holy Spirit were chosen to fulfill the daily task of feeding widows among the family of believers (Acts 6:1–6).

Some special widows attracted God's particular attention. Jesus took notice of a poor widow who gave two small coins to the temple treasury: "I tell you the truth," Jesus said, "this poor widow has put more into the treasury than all the others. They all gave out of their wealth; but she, out of her poverty, put in everything—all she had to live on" (Mark 12:43–44).

Centuries before, another nameless widow found the special favor of God. She was a Gentile from the town of Zarephath (near Sidon). She, too, warrants Jesus' mention in the Gospels (see Luke 4:25–26). God directed the prophet Elijah to this widow's home at the precise moment that she was baking her last morsel of flour and the dregs of her oil vessel into one last cake for her son and herself. In a test of faith, Elijah asked that she bake that cake for him, instead. Because she agreed to do so and also took Elijah into her home, the woman's flour and oil did not run out through more than three years of famine. God miraculously provided enough food for the woman, her only son, and His prophet. Later, when the woman's son became gravely ill and died, the prophet Elijah interceded with God on her behalf, and the son was restored to life.

The apostle Paul gave his protégé Timothy a list of qualifications for a godly widow: She is to be "well known for her good deeds, such as bringing up children, showing hospitality, washing the feet of the saints, helping those in trouble and devoting herself to all kinds of good deeds" (1 Timothy 5:10). Those widows to whom God paid special attention demonstrated many of these traits. Think of the prophetess Anna or Ruth the Moabite or Nabal's widow, Abigail. Think, too, of the two women whose stories we've just read: the widow of Zarephath and the widow Jesus noticed in the temple. These women willingly gave all they had in obedience to God. Because of this selflessness, they did not go unnoticed in His eyes. Oh, to have had the privilege of being noticed by Immanuel—the incarnate Christ who chose to be with us.

The great comfort is that widows need not remain stranded in the icy tundra of desolation and isolation. Through God's often-miraculous provision and through their own selfless actions, they can find belonging, assistance, and worth within the body of Christ. It's not only widows who feel abandoned on the roof of the world—and not only widows who can experience the security of being rescued by the warm arms of a loving God.

God, when I feel most alone, comfort me with Your presence. Then equip me to carry Your comfort to those on the precipice of despair. Amen.

49

SERVANT:
AN ATTENDANT

His master replied, "Well done, good and
faithful servant! You have been faithful with a
few things; I will put you in charge of many
things. Come and share your master's happiness!" (Matthew 25:21)

My first "real" job as a teenager was as a server. I
worked for a Christian family who owned a
catering service. Each Saturday afternoon, they
would pack their van with all the necessities: main
course, hors d'oeuvres, vegetables, coffee, punch,
rolls, table settings, serving pieces, and more. Then
they would swing by my house to pick me up. Out
I would trot bedecked in my lacy white blouse and
skirt, complemented nicely by my freshly polished
white tennis shoes. And we'd be off to serve at a
church banquet, anniversary celebration, or wedding reception.

My most humiliating moment (at least to that
point in life) came as I was preparing to serve a
wedding reception. It was a humid summer afternoon when we set up shop in the basement of a
church. The polished gray cement floors were coated
with a fine, clammy mist. After we had unpacked
our gear, I set the tables, put out the punch bowl,
and mixed the sweet red liquid.

Although all the invited guests would serve
themselves punch, I thought it would be nice to
provide the bridal party with glasses of refreshing

punch on the head table. Just before the guests were to arrive, I located a metal cart, lined it with glasses, and carefully filled them with punch. No sooner had I started pushing the cart toward the head table, then my rubber-clad foot caught the slimy cement the wrong way, slid into the cart's back wheel, and sent fourteen glasses of red punch tumbling onto the front of my white lace blouse. My boss heard the commotion (metal carts and glass make a clamor crashing onto a cement floor) and came running to my aid. Although I had to serve guests that evening wearing a red lace blouse, Sharon taught me the true meaning of serving as she comforted, soothed, and forgave me.

Although servants get a bad rap in our culture, God (as usual) turns human thinking upside down. He highly values those with the hearts of servants. Jesus not only called His followers servants (Matthew 10:24; 24:45–46; 25:21, etc.), but He lived out the perfect example of a servant—down to performing the filthy task of washing His disciples' feet during their last Passover meal together.

Paul told the Philippians they (and we) should have the same attitude as was in Jesus who "made himself nothing, taking the very nature of a servant" (Philippians 2:7). Serving, becoming an *attendant* in Christ's kingdom, requires an attitude of humility. It requires that we lay aside our own rights in deference to Him. We'll always find ourselves humbled as we serve—although not always as humorously as I was in the red punch incident.

The Greek and Hebrew words translated *servant* sometimes refer to someone forced into slavery, but more often to one "who gives himself up to another's will" or to "those whose service is used by Christ in extending and advancing His cause among men" and who are "devoted to another to the disregard of one's own interests."[1]

God calls Moses "my servant" numerous times, because Moses set aside his own best interests to attend to God's work. It was another attendant, the servant girl Rhoda (*a rose*) who answered Peter's knock when the angel miraculously released him from prison the night before he was to be executed (Acts 12:13–16). But one of the sweetest servant stories in all of Scripture comes from a little slave girl whose name we never learn.

She was an Israelite child, taken captive by Naaman, the commander of the king of Aram's army. She served Naaman's wife. She must have been a bright, attentive child, because she knew about the prophet Elisha and the miracles he was performing back in her homeland. So when she learned her master Naaman was afflicted with leprosy, the servant went to her mistress, telling her that there was a prophet in Israel who could bring wholeness to Naaman's body. The wife told her husband, who told the king, who sent Naaman to Joram, king of Israel—who panicked. Elisha heard this and sent for Naaman. When Naaman obeyed Elisha's mysterious command (dip seven times in the Jordan River), he was healed.

This little servant girl must have had a stellar track record. At her endorsement a military commander, two kings, a great prophet, and God Himself were moved to action. We see no indication that this child complained about being taken captive by a band of raiders, torn away from her family, and pressed into labor against her will. She didn't slack off amidst daily drudgery; she worked dutifully, as an example of how God's child ought to approach her work. And instead of becoming bitter, she felt compassion for her overseers, thus repaying her master with good.

God chose well when He assigned this child to a life of service in a foreign land, for the name of Jehovah, God of Israel, received great acclaim throughout Aram as the result of this child's compassionate expression of faith in Him.

I believe the day this girl passed into eternity she heard the words Jesus said would welcome His servants: "Well done, good and faithful servant! . . . Come and share your master's happiness!" (Matthew 25:21).

Master of the Universe: Thank You for the privilege of serving You. Help me live in such a way that one day You will call me Your faithful attendant. Amen.

NOTE
1. Thayer's definition of *doulos* from *The Online Bible Thayer's Greek Lexicon and Brown Driver & Briggs' Hebrew Lexicon* (Ontario, Canada: Woodside Bible Fellowship, 1993).

50

ADULTERESS:
INTIMATE ALLIANCE

> The woman said, "I know that Messiah"
> (called Christ) "is coming. When he comes, he
> will explain everything to us." Then Jesus
> declared, "I who speak to you am he." (*John*
> *4:25–26*)

It Could Happen to You was a hit movie a few years
ago. It told the story of a police officer who
promised half of the possible proceeds from his lot-
tery ticket to a waitress, in lieu of a tip. Funny thing
was, the ticket won millions of dollars. The officer
was true to his promise, giving the down-and-out
waitress half of the winnings. But his wife, por-
trayed as a nasty, cranky, spoiled money-grabber,
got progressively angrier at him for this kind gesture.

Audiences quickly found themselves rooting
for the officer to ditch his nasty wife and take up
with the sweet, sensitive waitress. The drama was
so convincing that the eventual adulterous relationship between the officer and the waitress felt like
the obvious action, whereas faithfulness within a
difficult marriage seemed like a ridiculously outdat-
ed convention.

Such is our culture. Wrong has become right,
and right has become wrong. But for Jesus (and
those who follow Him); sin is always sin, right is always right, wrong is always wrong. Nevertheless,
He was the least judgmental of any human who has

ever lived—although He had every right to be otherwise, as He was utterly without sin. One day He
will judge those who haven't responded to His mercy, but it was His mercy that was displayed during
His incarnation.

What would Jesus have told our waitress friend
about pursuing this adulterous relationship? We
have some hints in two recorded interactions between Jesus and adulterous women, women who
had chosen the wrong *intimate alliances*.

The first woman was dragged in front of Jesus
by a gaggle of sanctimonious Pharisees. "Here, Jesus. We caught this one in the act of adultery.
What're You gonna do with her?" At first, Jesus refused to answer, choosing to bend down and write
on the ground with His finger. When they persisted, Jesus stood up momentarily and said, "If any
one of you is without sin, let him be the first to
throw a stone at her" (John 8:7). Then He returned
to His sand writing. When He stood up again, He
was alone with the woman. He asked whether anyone was left to condemn her. She replied that none
of her accusers was left. She was alone with the
One who was without sin, but His next words are
interesting: "'Then neither do I condemn you,' Jesus declared. 'Go now and leave your life of sin'"
(John 8:11).

Jesus was straight with the woman: What
you've done is sin, but I know you are genuinely
penitent. I forgive you—but don't return to that
way of life ever again.

In another instance recorded by John, Jesus
carried on a long conversation with a Samaritan
woman who had been through five husbands and

was now living with a man who was not her husband. Jesus met her at a well and asked her for water. She was shocked that a Jewish man would even acknowledge her presence. They talked for a while about living water and husbands and true worship. She asked him questions. He answered her directly. Later she would tell her fellow townspeople, "He told me everything I ever did" (John 4:39).

The woman was trying to understand everything this strange man was telling her, but she wasn't quite getting it. Finally, she said, "I know that Messiah" (called Christ) "is coming. When he comes, he will explain everything to us" (John 4:25).

Jesus took this opening to tell her straight out—"I who speak to you am he" (John 4:26). No metaphorical description of Himself as "the Son of Man." No cryptic allusions to "My Father." Just, "You're expecting Messiah. Well, here I am!" At only one other point in the Gospels was Jesus so direct: when before His crucifixion the high priest asked Him: "Tell us if you are the Christ, the Son of God," and He replied, "Yes, it is as you say" (Matthew 26:63–64).

The woman who came to the well at midday, guilty and downtrodden because of her grievous sins, left the well transformed. She experienced freedom from her past because it was now in the open, a subject God knew about, one for which He would forgive her. It need never again be covered over in the shadows, spoken of in a guilty whisper. She was a new woman because she now had an intimate relationship with the Savior of the world.

She ran to town and brought all the people to

Jesus, saying: "Come, see a man who told me everything I ever did. Could this be the Christ?" (John 4:29). When the villagers came to Jesus, they listened to Him for two days. As He was leaving, they told the woman: "We no longer believe just because of what you said; now we have heard for ourselves, and we know that this man really is the Savior of the world" (John 4:42).

The shunned sinner became the welcomed missionary who was not content to keep the Messiah for herself, but she spread the news everywhere of His saving grace.

What would Jesus tell an adulteress (or an adulterer) today? From these two interactions, we can conclude that Jesus would say: "I am the Christ, the One with authority to forgive sins. I love you. I will forgive you, if you repent. I will free you from slavery to sin and make you clean. Leave your sin and *ally* yourself with Me, for I know you *intimately*. And bring all your friends along too. I have enough love, enough grace, enough forgiveness for everyone who comes to Me."

Jesus, thank You for Your marvelous expressions of grace, mercy, and forgiveness to these women—and to me. I do repent of my sins. I ask You to make me clean. With enthusiasm, now, I will go tell everyone who will listen of the wonderful freedom they, too, can find in You. Amen.

51

DAUGHTER:
BELOVED CHILD

Jesus turned and saw her. "Take heart, daughter," he said, "your faith has healed you." And the woman was healed from that moment. (*Matthew 9:22*)

Being a daughter has its distinct privileges. For me, it meant being Daddy's little girl. It meant an annual Daddy/daughter date on an autumn Saturday morning, when my Pioneer Girl leaders at South Park Church (Park Ridge, Illinois) prepared a pancake breakfast for us girls to serve to our dads. It meant summer afternoons when Dad's and my kites were the only two in the whole Windy City that never got off the ground. It meant evening Ping-Pong games, countless skinned knees that he hugged into feeling better, and many loose teeth that he wiggled out of my growing mouth.

Being a daughter also meant developing an ever-growing friendship with my mom. She had waited nearly nine years of married life for a child —and there I was, her only child. From when I was a tot, we did "friend" things together, Mom and I. As I got older, she and I sang together at mother/ daughter banquets, and she accompanied my violin solos at school and in church. Today, Mom and I still hold many common interests (especially *shopping!*) and often serve the Lord together in music ministry.

The Scriptures speak of many daughters. Some are daughters mentioned in relation with their parents; others are described only as daughters of God.

In Acts the writer mentions the four daughters of Philip the evangelist, who prophesied. All we know about them is that they were single adults and that they helped their father host the apostle Paul during one of his missionary journeys (Acts 21:8–9). Since the writer does not elaborate, either these four women were known to the early church or the author chose not to tell us any more. But these women have left a powerful legacy—God found them available and useful for His purposes. They didn't need to be married. They didn't need to perform mighty miracles. God spoke through these women at a crucial point in the history of the faith.

Then there was the Canaanite mother who begged Jesus to have mercy on her by releasing her daughter from demon possession (Matthew 15:22). Jesus responded to her insistent request by healing her daughter and by pronouncing the commendation: "Woman, you have great faith!" (Matthew 15:28).

Yet another New Testament daughter is the twelve-year-old only child of Jairus, a synagogue ruler. Jairus, a loving father, threw himself at Jesus' feet. His daughter lay dying, but in faith he pled with Jesus, "Come and put your hand on her, and she will live" (Matthew 9:18).

While Jesus was moving through the crushing crowd, on His way to raise up the daughter of Jairus, He felt a rush of power go out from Him. He stopped and scanned the crowd. He asked, "Who touched me?" (Luke 8:45). His disciples looked at Him like he was an alien. *What do You mean, who touched You? There are thousands of people pressing against You.* But He persisted.

I wonder what Jairus was thinking. If it were I, the thoughts would sound like this: *Come on, Jesus. My little girl is dying. Hurry up. Please. You said You'd come and heal her. We're going to be too late.*

Then a woman emerged from the crowd, and, "seeing that she could not go unnoticed, [she] came trembling and fell at his feet" (Luke 8:47). She poured out her story to the attentive Savior and to the crowd. She "had been subject to bleeding for twelve years, but no one could heal her" (8:43). She knew that if only she could touch the hem of Jesus' robe, she would be healed. The moment she touched Him, the bleeding stopped.

In Jewish culture, when a woman was hemorrhaging, she was considered unclean. No one could touch her without becoming unclean himself. She must have longed for the comfort of a husband's loving embrace or a daddy's hug. After such a loss of blood, she was also physically weak; every move was an effort. Mark's account also notes, "She had suffered a great deal under the care of many doctors and had spent all she had, yet instead of getting better she grew worse" (Mark 5:26).

Then she heard about Jesus. She knew she had to try this one more cure. Jesus was her last hope, just as He was Jairus's last hope.

Jesus, in His tender reply, did more than heal her physical body; He gave her worth and dignity by calling her "daughter." Not "woman," as He called the Canaanite mother. But "daughter." He accepted her into His family. He loved her, and that was why He offered her the gift of a healed body.

Jesus knew her pain. Although this woman's affliction was not a direct result of her sinfulness, it was one of the physical results of a sin-cursed universe. Jesus felt compassion for people suffering physically and did not always confine His ministry to spiritual healing. Isaiah 53:4 says, "Surely he took up our infirmities and carried our sorrows." This woman's suffering was among the burdens Jesus would bear in His body on the Cross. So Jesus dealt with her tenderly, kindly, yet firmly. He wouldn't let her keep this miracle to herself; yet He dignified her with a commendation, "Daughter, your faith has healed you. Go in peace and be freed from your suffering" (Mark 5:34).

Then Jesus turned and went to Jairus's house, where they found his daughter dead. Sending away a slew of ruthless mourners, Jesus brought the parents into the girl's room and raised her back to life.

The daughter of Jairus received her miracle, and the daughter of God who had been bleeding got her miracle. Just another day in the three-and-a-half-year earthly ministry of Jesus. But the families whose lives He touched would never be the same.

Like this little girl, many of us have been blessed in this life with loving parents; but how much more glorious it is that our souls can be set free by our loving heavenly Father through the touch of His only Son, Jesus.

Father, what a marvelous thought that because of Jesus You can call me Daughter. Thank You for the loving care and tenderness You offer my often bruised and weary soul. Grant me the faith of these, my sisters, that I may always trust You to meet my deepest needs. Amen.

52

CONCLUSION:
HER REWARD

> Give her the reward she has earned, and let
> her works bring her praise at the city gate.
> (*Proverbs 31:31*)

A woman's work is never done.
  Have you ever wondered whether your daily
work is worth the effort? You perform tasks in your
household, in the church, and perhaps in the workplace, faithfully going through the motions of
tedious repetition. No sooner do you dust and vacuum, then the dust and grime settle in again; no
sooner do you change your child's diaper, then it's
wet again; no sooner do you achieve your department's sales goal for this month, then next month's
goal looms large on the horizon.

The monotony can be mind-numbing and dis-
couraging.

But every once in a while someone notices a
job well done. Maybe your husband brags to his
mother in your presence that you keep a spotless
home; maybe your boss gives you a bonus for
meeting the goal.

Rewards. They let you know your work is
worth something to someone.

Several years ago, I wrote a magazine feature
article about a young woman named Mandy who
had struggled with depression and thoughts of sui-

cide. The article not only described Mandy's descent into depression, but it showcased the way God raised her above her circumstances. In preparation for the writing I interviewed Christian counselors and gathered facts on helping those who are depressed.

For my efforts, I received an award of merit from my peers. I was elated. (The framed award still graces my wall.) Months later, a counselor I had interviewed called my office. He had given a copy of the published article to his teenage daughter. Through reading about Mandy, his daughter recognized the same symptoms of depression in a high-school friend—and was able to get help for that girl. That was more of a reward than all the accolades my peers could ever give.

We work every day for the award of a paycheck or for the acknowledgment of other people, but what of eternal rewards? Which of our deeds merit eternal recognition from God Himself?

For the reward of eternal fellowship with God, none of us could qualify in and of ourselves. No list of accomplishments ever amassed could be nearly enough to gain us a moment's admission into His loving presence. But those of us who have asked to be covered by Christ's payment of our entrance fee (through His death on the cross to grant us forgiveness of sin) qualify for the reward through Him.

Christ knows about rewards. He not only offers them, but He has received them. Remember the line in the book of Hebrews: "Let us fix our eyes on Jesus, the author and perfecter of our faith, *who for the joy set before him* endured the cross, scorning its shame, and sat down at the right hand of the throne of God" (Hebrews 12:2, italics added). The joy of saving us from eternal destruction was what carried Christ through the unutterable shame and agony of His death on the cross. In a sense, we are part of Jesus' reward for obedience to His Father.

The Father has also given Jesus the reward of unparalleled honor: "Therefore God exalted him to the highest place and gave him the name that is above every name, that at the name of Jesus every knee should bow, in heaven and on earth and under the earth, and every tongue confess that Jesus Christ is Lord, to the glory of God the Father" (Philippians 2:9–11).

On numerous occasions throughout His life's ministry on earth, Jesus promised His followers (and thus those of us in succeeding generations who have received His forgiveness) untarnishable rewards for faithful service (Matthew 6:19–21). In His best-known recorded sermon, known to us as the Sermon on the Mount, He spoke of heavenly rewards: "Rejoice [at your sufferings] and be glad, because great is your reward in heaven" (Matthew 5:12). Later, He told another crowd: "But love your enemies, do good to them, and lend to them without expecting to get anything back. Then your reward will be great, and you will be sons of the Most High" (Luke 6:35).

Not only do we receive the reward of eternal life someday, not only do we get to be called children of God, but we also get some benefits in today's world.

In Luke 12:31 Jesus says: "But seek his kingdom, and these things will be given to you as well." What things? Food, drink, clothing, and all the other daily necessities—all provided from the hand of the loving Father.

What else do we get? Every-minute access to Him through prayer. A generous helping of His wisdom whenever we ask. His companionship, so that we are never alone. Constant guidance from the One who knows us better than we could ever know ourselves. And much, much more.

Perhaps my favorite of His earthly rewards comes from Jesus' words in Matthew 11:28–30: "Come to me, all you who are weary and burdened, and I will give you rest. Take my yoke upon you and learn from me, for I am gentle and humble in heart, and you will find rest for your souls. For my yoke is easy and my burden is light."

Anxious to work and often weary, we too crave the priceless reward of rest.

In Proverbs 31 we see a long list of actions and character traits of a woman of virtue. Over the centuries, this list has provided fodder for countless in-depth studies that have dissected this nearly unattainable woman whose example all women are to emulate. The chapter concludes with the admonition to all who would listen: "Give her the reward she has earned, and let her works bring her praise at the city gate" (v. 31).

The theme carries through the Old and New Testaments: Work diligently, believer in God, for He righteously and justly rewards those who honor Him. You will not be disappointed.

As we think back over the life lessons we've learned from women of the Bible, an apt response would be to ask ourselves: What work can I do in the time allotted to me that is worthy of the reward that counts in God's sight?

SELECTED SCRIPTURES

Moody Press, a ministry of Moody Bible Institute,
is designed for education, evangelization, and edification.
If we may assist you in knowing more about Christ
and the Christian life, please write us without obligation:
Moody Press, c/o MLM, Chicago, Illinois 60610.